Title: Prove It: Examining t
Author: Dr. Frank Harber
Copyright: 2021 by Frank H

ISBN: 978-1-953606-02-0

Published by: Engedi Publishing LLC, in the United States of America.

Unless otherwise noted, Bible passages are from the Holman Christian Standard Bible, copyright 1999, 2000, 2002, 2003 by Holman Bible Publishers, Nashville, Tennessee; all rights reserved.

PROVE

EXAMINING THE EVIDENCE OF GOD'S EXISTENCE

IT

FRANK HARBER PhD, JD

"Frank Harber possesses a unique gift: the ability to convey a compelling argument for theism in layman's terms. *Prove It* unfolds like a courtroom drama. Harber presents evidence like an attorney, written for a jury of common folk. His argument for the existence of God is carefully laid out in a manner that the average reader can comprehend. The book provides language to arm watercooler apologists with tools to defend their faith to friends who are skeptics, while validating their own beliefs. The author's two career paths augment each other as this Doctor of Theology defends his beliefs using courtroom prowess in a legal drama page-turner."

—*H. Edwin Young*, *Senior Pastor, Second Baptist Houston*

"God wants you to know Him and discover His purpose in your life. He has proven His presence and power in many ways, and Frank Harber clearly points us to the reality of existence and the way you can have a relationship with the God of the Universe."

—*Jack Graham*, *Senior Pastor, Prestonwood Baptist Church*

"Frank Harber combines his sharp pastoral and legal skills to prove God's existence in this well-researched book. As a former atheist, he believed that God was a myth—but through extensive research, he discovered that God's existence can be proved beyond any reasonable doubt. The 10 proofs he presents in these pages are detailed and persuasive. God has provided enough evidence to convince the willing, he writes. Your faith in God will be strengthened as you read these pages. I pray many unbelievers, or those who doubt, will come to know in a personal way the living God through faith in His Son, Jesus Christ."

—*James Robison*, *Founder and President, LIFE Outreach International Fort Worth, Texas*

"In *Prove It*, Frank Harber uses his background as an apologist and lawyer to present and prove the case for God. As a lawyer, he negates the arguments of naturalism, and as an apologist he presents strong proofs for design. This book belongs in the library of anyone looking for a solid book containing convincing evidence for the existence of God."

—**Robert Jeffress**, *Pastor, First Baptist Church, Dallas, Texas*

"Frank Harber's new apologetics book, *Prove It*, helps you find the answers you're seeking about the existence of God. Examining the case for God using the excitement and rationality of a courtroom, this book proves the reality of God beyond all reasonable doubt. I highly recommend this book for anyone seeking truth!"

—**Robert Morris**, *Senior Pastor, Gateway Church, Bestselling Author of The Blessed Life, Beyond Blessed, and Take the Day Off*

"A theoretical vignette of a jury trial opens each intriguing chapter in *Prove It–Examining the Evidence of God's Existence*, and that is the perfect scenario for Frank Harber. As a practicing attorney and minister of the Gospel, Frank dives deep into Biblical evidence to validate the magnificence and wonder of God's design."

—**Joni Lamb**, *Co-Founder, Daystar Television Network*

"My friend, Dr. Frank Harber has written a book that I would recommend be on every Christian's bookshelf, *Prove It–Examining the Evidence of God's Existence*, which is on my favorite subject of apologetics. Frank has written easy to follow chapters answering so many questions that both believers and unbelievers have with tremendous research. I thank God for this gift to the church and to the kingdom. May it be read widely!"

—**James Merritt**, *Senior Pastor of Cross Pointe Church*

"Two millennia ago Simon Peter challenged believers to "always be ready to give an answer for the hope that is within you." That is, Prove it! Frank Harber has the mind of an academician, the heart of an evangelist, and the passion of a lawyer. This new book should have a prominent place on the shelf of anyone and everyone who is serious about defending the faith they hold near and dear."

—O.S.Hawkins Ph.D., Author of the best selling "Code Series" including the Jesus Code and the Joshua Code

"If a judge and jury were asked to decide, would there be enough evidence to prove God's existence beyond a reasonable doubt? Absolutely! That's the journey Frank Harber takes us on in Prove It. Whether you are a skeptic in search of the truth or a believer who wants to be better equipped to answer questions about your faith, *Prove It* makes the case and delivers it in a series of helpful, informative presentations. You can see the evidence of Frank's hard work on every single page, and this is one courtroom drama whose verdict has ramifications for us all."

—Kevin Ezell, President, North American Mission Board, SBC

"The evidences Dr Harber provides is from the mind of a scholar and the heart of passion. As an attorney Dr. Harber makes his case by clear biblical and historical truth. Read and better know how to defend your precious faith."

—Dr. Johnny Hunt, Senior Vice President of Evangelism and Leadership for the North American Mission Board

"Frank Harber has written a timely book to challenge the belief systems accepted by so many today. I urge you to read this, believe it and then apply the truths!"

—Gary Frazier, Ph.D., President Discovery Ministries

"No one can make a compelling case quite like Dr. Frank Harber. In a culture where the existence of God is on trial everywhere you look, Frank makes an airtight case for faith with irrefutable evidence. Having trained hundreds of thousands of students and youth leaders, in leadership, over many years I find this book to be a book I wish I had available before now. Every student, every leader, every Pastor should grab a copy. "

—**Dr. Jay Strack**, *Founder & President of Student Leadership UniversityHost- "There's Always a Way" Podcast*

"Pastor, evangelist, apologist, attorney—God has given Dr. Frank Harber numerous gifts to engage atheists, agnostics, skeptics and seekers. Purchase multiple copies of this powerful resource and let my good friend, Dr. Harber, teach and equip you to share Jesus Christ with passion, compassion, and confidence. I believe this book will be used mightily by God in changing many eternal destinies from hell to heaven, and that excites me!"

—**Dr. Danny Forshee**, *Pastor Great Hills Baptist Church, Austin, Texas*

"This book is a must read for the Christian and a must gift for the skeptical friend. Dr. Frank Harber uses illustrations, Biblical evidences, scientific information, philosophical axioms, and natural processes in order to weave a tapestry of evidences that strongly refutes every idea that God does not exist. This is a most timely work that is greatly needed for the challenging times in which we live. It inspires and informs honest inquiry by those who honestly seek answers to life's greatest questions about God."

—**Malcolm McDow**, *Senior Professor of Evangelism (Ret.), Southwestern Baptist Theological Seminary, Fort Worth, Texas*

"Dr. Frank Harber is to be commended for his timely book, *Prove It– Examining the Evidence of God's Existence.* As a former atheist, he understands the challenges that face the church as we try to engage a world that is spiraling deeper every day into secular humanism, radical socialism, and rampant hedonism. As a result, more than ever Christians must be prepared to explain their faith and to give a reasonable defense for what they believe. That is why Frank wrote the book. I strongly encourage you to get a copy soon and absorb every page!"

—*Dr. David A. Wheeler, Professor of Evangelism, Sr. Executive Director of LU Shepherd Rawlings School of Divinity*

"Helping today's generation navigate the questions many have about God is critically important. I so appreciate how Frank Harber does this in his compelling new book. As a pastor I'm thankful for this tremendous resource as we share the hope of Jesus with our world."

—*Dr. Brad Jurkovich, Senior Pastor, First Baptist Church Bossier City, LA*

"There is no more important decision to be made by anyone than whether God exists. Frank Harber does a masterful job of demonstrating that there is no need to check your intellect at the door to believe in God. And he does it in a way that reads like an exciting legal novel! You will enjoy this book but more importantly you need this book. And so does everyone you know. After you read it, the verdict will be crystal clear!"

—*Dr. John Avant, President of Life Action*

"I've known Frank since the early 1990s – what a gifted communicator and apologist of God's Truth! Glad to call him my 'Forever Friend'. And so thankful for his new book, *Prove It!*"

—*Dennis Swanberg, America's Minister of Encouragement*

"Court is in session! In Prove It, Dr. Frank Harber leverages his training as an accomplished apologist and lawyer to present and prove the case for God to you, his jury. Readers, beware! If you step into the jury box of Harber's courtroom, be prepared to deliver a verdict from the evidence he presents that atheism is guilty of fraud—in the first degree."

—*Dr. Matt Queen, Associate Professor and L. R. Scarborough Chair of Evangelism ("The Chair of Fire") Associate Dean of the Roy J. Fish School of Evangelism and Missions Southwestern Baptist Theological Seminary, Fort Worth, Texas*

"Frank Harber is uniquely equipped to write this book. His background as an atheist exposed him to the questions; his theological training equipped him with the answers; and his legal training armed him with how to convincingly argue them. From beginning to end, *Prove It* delivers. Harber cogently and credibly dismantles opposing arguments, disrobing objections that have been disguised as scientific truth. This book doesn't just preach to the choir. It is creative, informative, entertaining, and attention-sustaining. Best of all, it's persuasive. Ultimately, Harber demonstrates that believing in God is not only true beyond a reasonable doubt, it is sustained by a pre-ponderance of evidence. Read this book for your own encouragement or buy a copy for a skeptic or doubting friend. The believer's faith will be confirmed and the skeptic's doubts will be confounded."

—*Deron Biles, Professor of Preaching, Southwestern Baptist Theological Seminary, Fort Worth, Texas*

"I have known Frank Harber all his Christian life. I have always been impressed with his ability to combine his keen intellect with spiritual truth. You undoubtedly will be profited by reading this book."

—*Reverend Bruce Wells, Retired*

"BRILLIANT JUST BRILLIANT! If you question God's Existence, this book was written for you."

—*Jeff Audas, Big Vision Advisors, Co-Founder Team Impact*

"My friend Frank Harber has a unique gift of explaining and teaching really complex truths in a very tangible and understandable way. That is why I am so excited about Frank's new book, *Prove It–Examining the Evidence of God's Existence*. This is a must have for any follower of Jesus who is wanting to understand their own faith, and has the desire to share their faith with others. Grab a copy for yourself, and one for a friend that is searching for truth."

—*Shane Pruitt, National Next Gen Director – North American Mission Board (NAMB), & Author of 9 Common Lies Christians Believe*

"Frank Harber is a master of apologetics and is uniquely qualified to speak to this matter as a former atheist who became a Christian, Bible Scholar and Pastor after discovering Christ in a journey to disprove Him. If you are grappling with the idea of God or need more facts to defend your faith, this book is a great place to start!"

—*Jonathan Lamb, Daystar Television*

"Frank Harber has produced a creative and stimulating apologetics resource that deserves wide circulation. He creatively presents the evidence for the existence of God in a way that will challenge, and hopefully convince, the most committed skeptic. I know it will inform, edify, and prepare believers to live boldly and confidently share the hope that is within them. Observing the chaotic conditions of modern-day life, I am convinced this is an important book to read and share."

—*Ken Hemphill, Former President of Southwestern Baptist Theological Seminary and National Strategist for Empowering Kingdom Growth.*

"Frank Harber uses the brilliance of a lawyer and the urgency of an evangelist to get a verdict for belief in the God of the Bible. Using historical data, scientific facts, reason and logic Frank points people to scriptural truth. When you start reading it, you will not want to put it down."

—*Dr. Jim Richards, Southern Baptists of Texas Convention*

"In his book, *Prove It – Examining the Evidence of God's Existence*, Dr. Frank Harber provides convincing evidence concerning the existence of God. He negates the philosophical platitudes that counter Christianity and refutes scientific arguments, which tell us that there is no proof of God. As a skilled lawyer, he systematically dissects the arguments of naturalism and responds with sound evidence for Design. Both Christian and non-Christian students need to read this work. Pastors should teach these great truths to their congregations. Prove It is a fantastic resource and is desperately needed at this moment of history. Open your heart. Open your mind. The proof is there!"

—*Dr. Sammy Tippit, Author and International Evangelist*

"From both a theological and a legal background, Frank Harber, sets out not only to prove the existence of God, but to show why it matters. Ten chapters, present in a legal, defensive, format why one should believe in God. Readers are asked to be the jury. Especially helpful information appears in the Epilogue, "Reaching a Verdict" where Harber presents four simple truths on which to bet your life. An outstanding book, that ought to be read by believer and non-believer alike."

—*Dr. Dan R. Crawford, Senior Professor of Evangelism & Missions, Chair of Prayer Emeritus, Southwestern Baptist Theological Seminary, Fort Worth, Texas.*

"Few times in life do you meet true gifted and talented men like Frank Harber. His mentorship, his academic pursuit and his theological perspectives are not only sound in doctrine according to scripture, but they are profound with a supernatural anointing from the Holy Spirit. When you delve deep into this book, do yourself a favor. Read what is written, and then allow God to give you insights and perspective from the subtext. As a filmmaker working around this industry, we seek out storyteller's who understand subtext. You will be challenged in your faith and this is an honor to stand alongside of this man of God, who continues to ask the hard questions from a "unique worldview". His love of Jesus is unquestioned. "

—*Kevin McAfee, Film Producer and Director, Known for Beyond the Gates of Splendor (2002), End of the Spear (2005) and Last Ounce of Courage (2012)*

"I highly recommend this outstanding book! It will strengthen the faith of any believer, and it can also be used as a powerful evangelistic tool as it presents rational, easily understood reasons for believing in the existence of God."

—*Dr. Ken Alford, Former President of the Florida Baptist Convention, and former Chairman of Trustees of the Southern Baptist Convention's North American Mission Board*

"This book is fantastic! Frank Harber shows us the evidence and calls us to an informed faith. Never has apologetics been more important than in this generation. *Prove It* allows us to examine the evidence for ourselves and to see that there is a God who cares deeply about us. Get this powerful book!"

—*Doug Munton, Ph.D., Author, Adjunct Seminary Professor, Senior Pastor, FBC O'Fallon, IL*

"The question persists through every generation of human experience: Does God exist? How one answers this question will shape the answer to all other questions in life. In *Prove It*, Frank's education and experience in both law and theology come together to present compelling evidence for God's existence. He brilliantly weaves together popular illustration, dynamic evaluation, conversational interaction, biblical evidence, and historical confirmation to confront the most common challenges to this question of all questions. His presentation of the evidence for God is both gracious and clear, compelling and kind. I encourage you to read with full expectation that your deepest questions on God's existence may actually have answers, and that you might just find those answers in these pages."

—*Tony Wolfe, Southern Baptists of Texas Convention*

"Engaging, compelling, biblical, and theological are all terms describing Dr. Frank Harber's masterful treatment of skeptics' question, "Does God exists?" He rightly underscores that "the Bible doesn't need to convince us God exists...," yet judiciously highlights the establishment of principles in the earth, revealing God's existence. After reading this insightful work, prepare yourself to render the overwhelming verdict, "It's proven, God does exist!"

—*Carl J. Bradford, Assistant Professor of Evangelism, Roy Fish School of Evangelism & Missions*

"Some skeptics assert that belief in God is irrational. Frank Harber, trained theologian and practicing attorney, begs to differ! Through the use of several "courtroom scenes," Harber presents and analyzes evidence for the existence of God. I believe he has proved his case. Read this book! I think you will agree."

—*Timothy K. Beougher, Ph.D. Associate Dean, Billy Graham School of Missions, Evangelism and Ministry, Billy Graham Professor of Evangelism and Church Growth*

"Some say that faith in God is a blind leap or an example of wishful thinking. But it is not! Faith is reasonable. There are overwhelmingly compelling reasons for believing that the God of the Bible is real, and that Jesus Christ really is the Son of God. I, like Dr. Harber, came to faith after years of atheism. I was a skeptic, but when faced with the evidence for faith, my life was forever changed. I challenge you to pick up this book and dare to doubt your doubts and consider the reasons for believing in the God who made you and loves you."

—*Dr. Greg Faulls*, *Senior Pastor, Bellevue Baptist Church, Owensboro, Kentucky and Assistant Professor, John W. Rawlings School of Divinity, Liberty University*

Dedication

This book is dedicated to:

My wife Becky and our four children Graham, Gabrielle, Hunter and Hannah.

Contents

Foreword

When I first wrote *Evidence that Demands a Verdict* more than thirty years ago, I had just come along a journey very similar to Frank Harber's. As a young man and an atheist, I just knew I could be the first person ever to prove conclusively that God does not exist. After my analysis, no longer would religious ramblings gain any traction in rational debate among human beings. It was a goal so invigorating that I researched, studied, and analyzed more resolutely than I had anything in my life to that point. What I discovered disappointed my larger-than-life ambitions, but it saved my eternal soul.

God does exist. He is palpably obvious to anyone who will consider the evidence with even a shred of intellectual honesty. If you have any doubt that he is this clearly revealed to us, then you are holding the book that will sweep the questions away.

Frank Harber was once what I was: a hard-edged atheist with a self-imposed duty to himself and mankind to disprove the "God myth." But alas, poor atheist, he discovered the same unyielding reality that I did. Not only can God not be disproved, he can very well be proved—even when subjected to standards as exacting as those required by legal examination.

Frank has done a masterful job of presenting his evidence in this book. As much as anything I've ever taught, what he writes still demands a verdict of anyone willing to consider what he has to say.

If you are a devoted believer, this imaginative presentation of the ten greatest proofs of God will fortify your faith in a lively new way, and it will prepare you to tell others more confidently than ever just how clearly God has made himself known. On the other extreme, if you are an unbeliever craving some way to be sure God is not, I applaud your courage in picking up this book. Be bold enough to go wherever it takes you.

To anyone's demand that someone "prove God"—no matter how arrogantly or skeptically the challenge is thrown out—I say that Frank Harber has.

—*Josh McDowell*

Acknowledgments

This book would not have been possible without some special people in my life.

Thank you Pastor Bruce Wells for leading me to Christ when I was a skeptic. You introduced me to apologetics. Thank you for urging me to attend Southwestern Baptist Theological Seminary in Fort Worth, Texas.

Thank you to my wonderful professors at Southwestern Baptist Theological Seminary for teaching me theology. You taught me Greek and Hebrew. You taught me how to be a theologian. You taught me about the great medieval thinkers like Thomas Aquinas. Professors Roy Fish and Malcolm McDow taught me evangelism. As a student and later a professor, Southwestern has always been home. Thank you to former President Ken Hemphill who co-wrote the GotLife apologetics and evangelism resources with me. My former student, Adam Greenway is now the 9th President of Southwestern. He is a great apologist and will lead the Seminary in reaching this ever-increasing skeptical generation.

Special credit goes to the late Zig Ziglar who encouraged me to do this project. This book would not exist without Zig pushing me to write. His frequent calls of encouragement meant so much to me. This book would have never been finished without the weekly encouragement I received from Zig. He passed on knowledge to me that is priceless. Although Zig is now in heaven, knowing that he was the first person to ever read this book makes me smile.

Thank you to my wonderful friend Duncan Brannan. He is a great apologist. The courtroom dramas were inspired by his creative mind. He had an enormous role in inspiring this book. There is no end to his creativity!

Thank you to Andy Spencer. You revived this book and made it happen. His talent knows no limits. I am inspired every time I speak to him. I am humbled and honored to work with Andy on this wonderful book. Andy, you are amazing!

Finally, thank you to Texas A&M School of Law. Thank you to all my wonderful professors who taught and mentored me. I am proud to be a member of the first graduating class of Texas A&M University School of Law.

Order from the Court

COURTROOM DRAMAS fascinate us. Notorious trials dominate headlines for months at a time—think of Michael Jackson, O. J. Simpson, or Scott Peterson. Hours of media coverage and countless front-page stories feed the desire of people to know what really happened.

But why does a courtroom setting make us think the judge and jury will solve the mystery? What is the difference between a legal investigation and a casual inquiry into an event? Why do we feel assured that those involved will get to the bottom of the issue and find out who really did what? In the end, much of the allure of a trial is the promise of finding out the truth.

Whether the trial is a civil or criminal case, the assurance of *finding truth comes* from the process by which a legal hearing scrutinizes evidence for the claims on each side. In a courtroom, logical arguments for or against a proposition are examined dispassionately so a group of objective observers (the jury) can come to a reasonable conclusion about what happened, who is at fault, or who committed the crime. Presented clearly and orderly, the facts of a case explain the events and the roles of the people involved. Enough evidence must be presented to allow a jury to decide whether or not Michael Jackson harmed his young guests or Scott Peterson killed his pregnant wife.

Further, once the rational arguments are made, lawyers must present the facts in a way that the jury reaches the right conclusion. For this, too, legal proceedings offer a well-thought-out approach. Courts apply what are known as standards of proof to determine guilt or liability. Although these standards vary depending on the nature of the case being tried, a common criterion is that, to convict someone, evidence must show the accusation of guilt is true beyond a reasonable doubt. In other words, if a rational, intelligent person evaluates the facts presented, the only reasonable conclusion would be to believe the defendant is guilty of the crime as charged.

Notice, though, what the standard does not require. The benchmark is not that no doubt whatsoever exists. A case is proven if there is simply no reason to question seriously the accusation any further. Sure, the jury could second-guess the prosecutor, wonder what else might have happened under other circumstances, or merely be stubborn about not wanting to conclude what the facts suggest, but none of these are reasonable conclusions. Anyone can doubt something for no reason at all if he or she simply wants to disbelieve it—even if to do so is unreasonable. But the prosecution or defense does not have to eliminate all of the extraneous, illogical possibilities. The evidence simply must show why the explanation offered is the most likely conclusion—why no other interpretation makes sense.

While most people will never confront a jury to determine their future, each person faces an issue that determines everything else about how he or she will live. Yet, many people let presuppositions, popular notions, cultural fads, or incoherent thinking determine this most crucial question about how they go through life. Many assume it doesn't matter very much whether or not there is a God. But whether or not he is is the most important conclusion anyone will ever come to about anything.

That's why, in this book, I examine the case for God using the drama, fascination, and rationality of a courtroom. Although some people try to undermine the idea of a supreme being by saying that believing in God requires blind faith, instead, the opposite is actually true. As we apply the logic and power of evidence as in a trial, we will be amazed—and possibly excited—to see that God's existence can be confirmed beyond any reasonable doubt.

Will all possibility of questioning be erased? No more so than in a legal proceeding. The following pages present in two ways why believing in God makes much sense. Each chapter opens with a theoretical vignette, portraying what it would be like to watch a jury trial in which opposing parties debate whether or not God exists. Then the chapters flesh out a deeper understanding of each of ten great reasons to believe.

In our legal proceedings, the prosecution represents the doubters of God while the defense stands on behalf of believers. This is not to suggest either that God is on trial or that he needs to prove himself to anyone. In truth, the debate could be structured with either side as defense or prosecution. In our case (so to speak), I merely offer a scenario that makes it easier to present the facts. There is great evidence for God. It's the no-God position that's built on conjecture, presupposition, and wishful thinking, not evidence. And by the way, in this scenario, readers have to decide what to think—they're the jury.

CHAPTER ONE

Innate Desires Point to God

Prosecutor: *Your Honor, the prosecution objects to the Bible as evidence and moves to strike any reference to it from the court.*

Judge: *On what grounds, counsel?*

Prosecutor: *Best evidence, Your Honor. The defense has stated it cannot produce the original autographs. Without them, there is no way of verifying the Bible's credibility.*

Defense Attorney: *Your Honor, the Bible meets several qualifications under the hearsay rule. It's recorded by those with personal knowledge. It's trustworthy. It's an authentic document more than twenty years old. Its veracity is substantiated by profound discoveries such as the Dead Sea Scrolls and more than twenty-four thousand New Testament manuscripts, biblical passages containing detailed scientific and medical data.*

Judge: *Agreed. The objection is overruled. The Bible can be admitted into evidence, but prosecution may still examine its integrity or use it to impeach. Now, let's move on.*

Did you know that, among everything the Bible has to say about God, it never takes on the fight of trying to prove he exists? From beginning to end, the Bible tells the story of a world (ours) in which God is present. He made it. He runs it. The Bible assumes God exists. Christian Scripture tells us everything we need to know about this God, but it doesn't spend time trying to convince us that he is.

Have you ever wondered why?

The primary reason is that the Bible doesn't need to convince us God exists because God has created a universe through which his existence is so obvious that we require a Bible only to explain his purpose for our lives. Rational argument and a reasonable interpretation of what we see around us can make the reality of God clear. We are as surrounded by evidence of God as we are surrounded by air. In fact, air is a good place to start with our proofs of God. Let me explain.

For the Love of Air Tanks

There's a humorous story about a scuba diver who strapped on an air tank and dove enthusiastically into the Caribbean. About twenty feet down, he came upon a stunning school of colorful fish, but his serenity was interrupted by the presence of another diver. Oddly, the man had no air tank. Thinking the waters now a bit too crowded, the first diver dropped another fifteen feet. Once again, his enjoyment of the fish was disrupted by the tankless diver. Frustrated by the man's discourtesy, the man in scuba gear descended fifteen more feet but was quickly distracted again by the other guy. Finally he admitted to himself, "It's pretty amazing that fellow can dive this deep without an air tank." So, while still feeling a bit put out, the first diver wrote a message on his waterproof writing pad and held it toward the second: "How are you diving way down here without an air tank?" At that, the man snatched the board and scribbled what should have been the obvious answer: "Because I'm drowning, you idiot! Help me!"

Air tanks are crucial to scuba divers because they allow them to breathe in places people were not designed to breathe. Although we may never think of it, breathing is the greatest desire we have in life. It takes concentration and a force of will to hold one's breath for a single minute, and even the most practiced can last only a few minutes without taking a breath. We recognize how deep-seated this desire is only when we stop breathing. Otherwise, we take air for granted. But the desire is there all the time.

Each of us takes roughly 21,600 breaths a day to supply our bodies with its requirement of eighty-eight pounds of oxygen. That means every twenty-four hours, the body brings in two thousand gallons of air to meet with the four and one-half gallons of blood it pumps through the lungs. The body is remarkably geared to meet the desire for air. Normal breathing is about twelve times a minute, but when we run hard or do anything that raises the heart rate, we can breathe up to eighty times per minute. There are fifteen hundred miles of airways in the lungs, and more than 750 million alveoli, tiny air sacs through which oxygen is transferred to the blood. If we could spread out the air sacs in an average adult's lungs, they would cover one-third of a tennis court. On top of that, unless something is drastically wrong, every person is born knowing how to breathe. When we breathe, we exchange bad gas (carbon dioxide) for good gas (oxygen). Our cells need oxygen like a television needs electricity. That's why breathing is one of the most consistent needs we have, and as with all genuine needs, we also have an intense desire to meet it.

The Two Desires

Every human being's built-in desire to breathe is just one of several such desires with which we're all acquainted. In his wonderful book *The Weight of Glory*, the great twentieth-century Christian thinker C. S. Lewis explained the implications of what it means to desire something. Describing why our desires imply that God exists, he presented what is called the argument from desire.

Lewis noted there are two kinds of desires in life—innate desires and artificial desires. Innate desires are inborn, native, or inherent within us. Every human being who has ever lived has them. I've already described the innate desire to breathe. Another innate desire is to eat. Hunger reminds us that we are born with that need. Likewise, thirst is innate. So is sleep. And with each of these desires, there is a way to satisfy it. For eating, there is food. For drinking, there is water. For sleep, there is the act of sleeping. Each of these appetites corresponds to a real object or a way to satisfy the desire. The pattern is obvious: if we have an innate desire for something, there is a way to fulfill that desire.

There are also innate desires that are less tangible. People have the desire for knowledge, for fellowship with other humans, to experience beauty. And even for these desires, we find there are ways to meet the yearning. We can learn, socialize with other people, and see beautiful scenery or hear beautiful music.

Artificial desire, on the other hand, is quite different. An artificial desire comes from society, from advertising, or from some form of fiction or fantasy. Some of these desires are more real than others. For some people with a passion for speed, for instance, there are such things as sports cars to fulfill that spot in one's heart. But some artificial desires aren't quite based in reality. Someone might want to fly like Superman, but the way to satisfy that simply doesn't exist. Satisfying artificial desires is not always possible, and even if it is, the fulfillment may not be attainable (I still don't have a Corvette).

Unlike artificial desires, no one has ever found—not even one case!—an innate desire for a nonexistent object. Wouldn't it be terrible if you were hungry your whole life, and there were no such thing as food? A forever rumbling stomach and nothing you could do about it! Fortunately, as we look around, we find a satisfier for every innate desire, and that has some remarkable implications for why we know there's a God.

The Message in Desire

C. S. Lewis highlighted another innate desire that presents an unusual challenge—the desire for eternity, the yearning to live forever. At first glance, there doesn't seem to be any way to satisfy this passion, yet it is as much a part of us as our desire to breathe. Lewis argued that the rule still applies—there is something that can meet this innate desire, and it forces us to consider what the longing for eternity means. Since every innate desire corresponds to a real object, there must be something that can satisfy this desire for eternity. If it's not readily available on Earth's menu, where do we find the satisfier? Answering questions like that is what the Bible does best.

In Ecclesiastes 3:11a, Solomon observed that God "has made everything appropriate in its time. He has also put eternity in their hearts."

God has written a message within us. That's what Solomon meant when he said God has "put eternity in their hearts." The craving for eternity is hardwired into our systems, and this desire points us to God.

Blaise Pascal said, "In every person is a God-shaped size hole. A God-shaped size vacuum that only God can fill." Augustine said, "Our hearts are restless until they find their rest in God." To return to our logic of desire, then, we reason the other direction when it comes to this desire for eternity. Only an eternal God can offer eternity to us, so our desire must be directing us to that thing—God—that can satisfy the longing. Eternity is possible, but only because there is an eternal God who made it so. The desire for eternity evidences the reality of it as well as the God who is eternal.

Missing the Message

Although this particular desire can be met only by the God who put it in people, many folks try to fulfill it with things that can't satisfy. The truth is, we are all looking for something. Everyone we will ever meet is a driven person—some motivated by anger, some by guilt, others by shame, a few by a controlling parent. But perhaps one of the most common drives in our culture is materialism. Oddly enough, people try to fulfill the desires of their hearts with various physical things. It's like trying to satiate one's hunger by breathing. Or like feeling really thirsty, so we try to get some sleep.

Economic studies show that most family fortunes are dissipated within one generation of the person who amassed the fortune. Do you know why? Because when heirs get the money, they use it to fund a futile attempt to satisfy the desire they have for God. They spend immense sums, hoping to satisfy this longing, but the yearning remains because having and doing "stuff" doesn't achieve eternity.

Centuries before Christ, Plato recognized this problem. He said humans are like jars—for some reason, always partly empty. The renowned poet and playwright Oscar Wilde observed that there are two tragedies in life: one is not getting what you want, and the other is getting it. Many people are like that. They achieve their goals only to discover the success doesn't make them happy. They end up still empty.

This attempt to satisfy the desire for eternity—for God—in all the wrong ways has throughout history accompanied the emptiness. Alexander the Great conquered the known world as a young man, but it didn't satisfy him. In frustration, he died from a life of debauchery. The wealth of the military genius Hannibal was almost inconceivable. By his sweeping conquests he filled three bushel baskets with gold rings of the kings he had killed, but he died in a foreign land where not a single person wept for him.

The desire-based argument for the existence of God has been used by Christians for centuries—for example, Augustine, Pascal and, of course, C. S. Lewis. Pascal wrote, "If man were not made for God, why is man only happy in God?" Every one of us desires something this world cannot provide.

In Lewis's *Mere Christianity*, he echoed the argument from desire: "If I find in myself a desire which no experience in this world can satisfy, the most probable explanation is that I was made for another world." [1] Yet despite the clarity of this reasoning, some people object to the argument for desire.

Objections!

Skeptics offer two primary objections to the argument from desire—one having to do with personal happiness, the other with the problems in our world.

Happy, Happy, Happy

Some say, "The argument doesn't apply to me because I am totally happy in this life."

Now the argument from desire, I will point out, does require some honesty from the person who hears it. Is it totally honest when someone says of this life: "I'm completely happy, totally content. I would never want anything different. In fact, it's never even crossed my mind to think I would want any more than this life has to offer. Besides that, I'm looking forward to dying and becoming worm food"? I doubt it.

When someone tells you he is unremittingly happy, he's likely not facing life with thorough honesty. If anyone says money (or pleasure or power) truly has made him content, he stands in great opposition to everyone who has ever lived. The unanimous testimony of all celebrated literature confirms the claim is simply not so. Atheist Bertrand Russell lamented: "The life of man is a long march through the night toward a goal which few can hope to reach and none may tarry long. One by one as they march our comrades vanish from sight, seized by the silent orders of omnipotent death. Brief and powerless is man's life. On him and all of his race the slow sure doom falls, penniless and dark, blind to good and evil, omnipotent matter rolls on its relentless way." [2]

Another atheist, Jean-Paul Sartre admitted, "There comes a time when one asks even of Shakespeare, even of Beethoven, is this all there is?" [3] Countless people arrive at a point in life when they ask the same question. The is-this-all-there-is problem points to God and walks right into the argument from desire.

A multitude of dissatisfied people have lived only according to what this life offers, ignoring the next, only to discover their path is dismally unsatisfying. Even gifted, brilliant people like Karl Marx, Machiavelli, Sigmund Freud, and Ernest Hemingway all died bitter and lonely men. After battling severe depression, Hemingway committed suicide. Marx, Machiavelli, Freud... they tried to satisfy a heavenly desire in an earthly way, but it never worked. People keep trying, somehow thinking they can satisfy an ultimate desire with this world's stuff. They don't seem to realize that if all others have bet every time and lost, it's a pretty foolish gamble. It's like stepping up to a plate at which everyone in history has struck out, but thinking somehow I'm going to be the one who will hit a home run. It's never, ever happened.

There's a great analogy here to the one-time "science" of alchemy. During the Middle Ages, people conducted chemical experiments to achieve what is called the transmutation of base metals into gold. And did they ever succeed? Of course not. In fact, many wasted their lives trying to discover the right process.

Chemists today look at these experiments and laugh. Alchemy wasn't science at all—merely wishful thinking. Today, though, many people spend their lives pursuing spiritual alchemy, trying to find satisfaction for ultimate things in temporary pursuits. But history records a 100 percent failure rate for this bad experiment.

Perfect Is as Perfect Does

The second objection to the argument from desire is to say, "I don't believe a perfect being exists because we live in an imperfect world. If our world is not perfect, how can there be a God?"

What this line of thinking actually suggests are two rather stunning admissions that bring us right back to the argument from desire. First, it admits a person can imagine a perfect world; and second, because the world can be imagined, it admits the possibility that a perfect world could exist.

So where did this image of a perfect world come from? Could perfection ever arise from our present world? Could random acts of evolution—which are not very kind, by the way (think: survival of the fittest)—produce a perfect world? Could the forces of nature do it? Hurricanes, tornadoes, and earthquakes seem to do more harm than good.

Or what about human beings? On average, nineteen wars rage at any given time on this planet. So is mankind improving this world? How's our progress in eliminating terrorism, tragedy, poverty, and crime? It's clear a perfect world is not coming about through us. The image and hope can come only through a perfect being.

I will grant a concession to those who argue that a perfect being would create an ideal world. A perfect being, it is reasonable to suggest, would make a world in which there is no pain, no suffering, and no death—only joy, peace, and fulfillment. Interestingly enough, that sort of world aligns exactly with God's idea because that's the kind of world he made.

Scripture explains that the first man and woman were placed in a Mesopotamian garden called Eden. They were given everything their hearts desired. Every day they could fellowship with God— they had a standing appointment entered on their Palm Pilots. What an unbelievable thing to talk face-to-face with God each and every day!

Besides that, the first people had all the food they could eat. Strolling the garden was like a walking buffet, like going on a cruise. Although I've never been on one, people tell me the best part of a cruise is that they can eat all the time. In the garden of Eden, folks were on a land cruise! After a while in the garden, however, the man and woman couldn't get past the idea that God had forbidden them to eat the fruit of one particular tree. They wouldn't accept that they couldn't be like God, so they messed up the perfect world God had made.

All manner of people have the same problem today. They want paradise without God, heaven without the Lord of heaven. That's because people have a latent desire to be their own god.

I encountered a rather blatant example of this once as I talked with a skeptic about the existence of God. The woman said to me, "I do believe in God. I just don't believe Jesus is God." When I asked if she thought Jesus was a historical person, she replied, "Yes." Was he a good person? "Yes." Do you believe he was a prophet? "Yes." Do you believe he was God?

"No! Because," she continued, "I just don't believe he *should* be God."

So I asked, "What about you? Do you think you should be God?"

She concluded, "That would be a good start."

What a confession! When we don't follow God, we try to retain the throne in our own lives. Adam and Eve established the pattern.

If we read the Bible from Genesis to Revelation, we see that God started with a perfect world. Man messed it up, and God redeemed the situation. The whole purpose of planet Earth is to redeem man back to God so we can spend eternity with God in heaven. Which brings us to the perfect world again: Heaven is now our hope of a perfect world.

The Bible says we cannot fathom what heaven will be like. The apostle Paul visited heaven and told us in 1 Corinthians 2:9 that we can't imagine a place as magnificent as heaven. Yet, the King of heaven offers to share his space. All we have to do to obtain paradise is subject ourselves to the King.

Many people don't like the terms of the arrangement, but that's the way it is. A perfect world is possible only with a perfect being, and we can have it solely by meeting his stipulations. The good news is that it will satisfy the desire for eternity.

Is Time Forever?

As I said earlier, the Bible doesn't try to prove God to us, but it does explain who we are in relationship to him and what our lack of eternity in the face of our desire for it is all about. Turning again to Solomon, in Ecclesiastes 3:11a, he said, "[God] has made everything appropriate in its time."

You and I have our own time to be here on Earth. Then there's eternity. Time and eternity are different, but a lot of people don't seem to realize how crucial it is to distinguish between them.

Let me use an analogy to explain the value of our time on Earth. Suppose your banker calls you with very good news. An anonymous donor, he explains, loves you so much that this donor is going to make a daily deposit of 86,400 pennies in your account. That's $864 each and every day. But there is a stipulation: you must spend all the money each day during the day on which you receive it. If you don't spend it, you lose it. At midnight your bank balance drops back to zero. You get out your calculator and decide this is a pretty good deal. Your $864 per day amounts to $6,000 a week. That, in turn, is $315,000 a year. Could you live off that? I certainly could!

But that's a pretend game. I'll tell you right now it ain't gonna happen to you—or me. On the other hand, there's something not so terribly unlike that that is real. You do have a donor. He's not anonymous, and he's providing something more valuable than money. If you could sell this item, you would be the richest person on the planet. What your donor gives you every single day is time. He donates 86,400 seconds a day to you, and you have to spend it every day. You can't save it up, and amazingly, every living person has the same amount of time to use. Whether you are rich or poor, the president of the United States, a celebrity, or a nobody, it does not matter. Everyone gets the same ration of time.

So what exactly is time? Perhaps the best definition I've heard is: Time is a stretch of duration in which things happen. The "things happen" part is what makes time so crucial. Intuitively, we know time matters. Being able to tell time, for instance, is important enough that we teach the skill even to our young children. What is more vital, though, is to recognize that while we tell time, time itself tells us something as well. Time has a message for every man, woman, and child on Earth, a crucial, life-changing memorandum. Time tells us that *we are temporary*.

The apostle Paul pointed in another way to the temporary nature of who we are on this earth. "Our bodies are a tent," he said (see 2 Cor. 5:1). Generally speaking, no one lives permanently in a tent. Tenting is a temporary thing. People don't go on lifelong camping trips. Paul was telling us that we—our physical selves—are not permanent fixtures in the universe. We will end. Living in a house implies permanence, whereas living in a tent does not.

The Desire for Permanence

The Bible says in John 14 that God is building a mansion for all of his children. When we build a house, it is permanent, and God says he will build us a house in heaven. A lot of people don't understand that they don't live this life properly. They live as if this life will go on forever, but the Bible tells us this life is just preparation for eternity—a dress rehearsal, we might say.

Solomon said in Ecclesiastes 7:2 that the fool does not contemplate death. In other words, he or she ignores the message coming from the desire for eternity.

Have you ever contemplated your death and the purpose of your life and made a conscious decision to live for eternity rather than merely for time? If you have, you've made a choice to respond in a healthy way to your desire for eternity. It means your desire for eternity can and will point to God.

That takes care of the future and our desire for it to go on forever. But is there something else that points to God here and now?

Of course there is. We'll talk about that next.

CHAPTER TWO

Conscience Whispers His Presence

Bailiff: *State your full name and occupation for the record.*

Expert Witness: *Robyn Marshall. I'm a special agent with the Behavioral Sciences Unit for the Federal Bureau of Investigation.*

Defense Attorney: *Agent Marshall, would you please explain to the court what exactly you do for the FBI?*

Witness: *I analyze crime scene evidence and produce a description of the perpetrator—I develop criminal profiles.*

Defense: *I understand that you've interviewed thousands of convicts and researched hundreds of cases to create new criminal models for the FBI. You've also played a key role in apprehending more than fifteen hundred criminals in the past eight years. Is that correct?*

Witness: *Yes. I've made it my life's goal to understand the criminal mind so as to bring as many as possible to justice.*

Defense: *From your extensive research and experience, what is your foremost observation about criminals?*

Witness: *That every one of them, every human being—regardless of race, culture, or religion—has a conscience, an innate knowledge of right and wrong and an undeniable impression that he should do what is right.*

Defense: *But people can act contrary to conscience, can they not?*

Witness: *Without question. Conscience holds authority over someone only if it convinces the person that he or she will ultimately answer for the wrongs done. I've seen in the worst of criminals exactly how this works. Deep down, people believe they can get away with just about anything.*

That is, until death stares them in the face. When that moment comes, you'll never convince anyone eternal judgment is merely an idea.

Defense: *Why is that, Agent Marshall?*

Witness: *Because, counsel, every criminal's conscience screams all the way to the death chamber that God is real, and the condemned is about to meet him.*

Have you ever heard of the "cone of silence"? In the popular 1960s sitcom *Get Smart*, it was a joke. When secret agent Smart held a confidential meeting with the Chief, the two men covered themselves under a plastic bubble that sounded more like an echo chamber than a silencer. For airline pilots in the 1960s and many years since, however, the cone of silence was not a joke but a lifesaver. The aircraft cone of silence has allowed safe travel for millions in the airspace over North America.

The cone was created by a radio beam. Planes maintained their courses by tracking along an invisible signal tracing the path they were to follow. If for some reason the pilot allowed his craft to veer to the right of his designated course, his monitor would sound and deliver a code signal *N*. If the plane wandered to the left, another noise accompanied the signal *A*. As long as the plane remained on the correct course, the mechanism stayed quiet, and it was every pilot's goal to keep his craft in the middle of this cone of silence.

In recent years, the Federal Aviation Administration (FAA) has upgraded navigation and air traffic control technology, investing more than $3 billion for software to make sure we can fly safely. Now, radar creates for each aircraft an invisible "cube in the sky" to keep planes from colliding and to make sure they arrive at their destinations. Although these days there are three signals for the pilot—*A* to monitor altitude, *C* to identify the plane's call sign, and *S* to define the air situation in the cube—the principles of the cone of silence were so simple and effective, they still apply. Stay in the cube, and you'll be OK. Deviate and an alert warns of danger. And the central, overriding goal of all this technology is to ensure one thing: that any of us can board a plane anywhere in the country and fly safely to the destination of our choosing.

The Cone of Silence Within

When discussing innate desires in the previous chapter, we recognized the correlation between observable needs—food, water, air—and the ways to meet those needs. Similarly, there are physical phenomena that point us toward unseen things that show how life is meant to be. If you attempt, for instance, to draw a straight line on a page without using a guide of any sort, you won't wind up with a truly straight line (especially if your art skills match mine). The lack of straightness is clear when you place a ruler on the page and use it to draw a line that really is straight. The ruler tells us our freehand line is actually full of wiggles, bumps, and bends.

But I mentioned "unseen things." Like the invisible cone of silence, people in all cultures, in every period of human history, have been aware there is a monitor in every person that churns up inner "noise" when someone goes off course morally. The system pings when a person lies, cheats, steals, lusts, kills, or otherwise wrongs his or her fellow human beings.

The time-honored term for this radio beam of the heart is conscience. The ancient Greek word for *conscience is suneidesis*, which literally means "knowledge with" or "coknowledge." A more contemporary definition of conscience explains it as a feeling. The point is, though, that we all—whether in Greece two millennia ago or in America today—identify something internal that informs us of right and wrong. The ubiquitous presence of this something internal raises the important question: Where did this beacon come from? Despite the readiness of many people to shrug off its importance, a serious examination shows the conscience to be a powerful indicator that God exists.

Conscience: The Source

Have you ever done something wrong and felt guilty about it? That is the conscience helping you. The Greek word I mentioned before calls it "knowledge." I like the implication of the Greek understanding because it suggests conscience is some sort of information inherent within us. The idea is that an inner software program directs our moral sensibilities.

Here we begin to see the implications the conscience has for the existence of a God. Computers don't self-generate software. It is installed in the hard drive by a programmer. That's why computers all over the world can run similar functions, communicate via the Internet, and operate businesses in Shanghai the same way they do in Seattle. To observe, then, that people every-where have concluded the same sorts of things to be morally good and another set of things to be morally bad suggests that we are all similarly programmed to know right from wrong, good from evil, lust from love, greed from generosity. So who is the programmer?

In a general sense, we could propose a Creator has done this. But the Bible is very specific about where the conscience comes from, and it offers a straightforward argument that God is, in fact, the source. Romans 2:15, speaking of the Gentiles, says they "show that the work of the law is written on their hearts. Their consciences testify in support of this, and their competing thoughts either accuse or excuse them." Note first, the Bible asserts that the conscience exists, and second, it testifies that this moral sense is imprinted on each of us. Some people have called this inner directional beam "the voice of God," but it is certainly a part of our inner "wiring" that reflects the way he wants things to be.

Notice that I said the conscience "reflects the way he wants things to be." This is where some people get off track in recognizing how the conscience points to God. Just as the FBI expert testified in our trial at the beginning of this chapter, people can violate the rules their consciences are telling them to obey. This doesn't mean the conscience is not real or not placed there consistently by a higher power. It simply means every man, woman, and child has the ability to ignore the conscience and do whatever they want to anyway. Criminals violate their consciences, and so does everyone else in one way or another.

Sometimes when I play golf, I'm paired with people I do not know, which I often find is a great witnessing opportunity. I regularly get with a bunch of guys who cuss from tee to hole and one fairway to the next. It's funny when we get toward the end of the round and someone finally thinks to ask me, "What do you do?" As soon as I tell them I am a pastor, the swear words stop. The guys tune back into their consciences and do the right thing.

Skeptics and the Socially Advantageous Conscience

Now and then, there's a clear example of how profitable it can be that people have consciences. Every city post office in the United States, for instance, has what is known as a conscience fund. This fund consists of money returned to the post office by people who have defrauded the government. If someone's conscience bothers him, and he wants to give money he knows deep down he owes the government, he can deposit it in this fund, no questions asked. Apparently, it works. According to government statistics, since 1811, $3.5 million have been placed into the United States conscience fund.

It's important to understand, though, how a skeptic perceives the social advantages—like a conscience fund—brought about by the presence of a conscience within each of us. Whereas Christians understand conscience as the horse that comes before the cart, skeptics argue the conscience has been developed over centuries of human evolution because of the social advantages that come from good behavior. In the course of human development, they say, actions that were not socially advantageous became taboo. There is no fundamental right or wrong, but people, in order to avoid being shunned, regularly began to practice socially acceptable behavior. Skeptics say criminals who rob, assault, murder, rape, and commit other heinous crimes are doing things we do not like, but they are not things that are objectively wrong. Rape is not socially advantageous, but honesty is. Killing innocent people is bad for social stability, but chaste family relationships are good. And so on. However, there is a problem with that view.

Even atheist Bertrand Russell admitted some things are wrong in and of themselves. He acknowledged, for instance, that cruelty to children fundamentally is wrong always. Russell agreed it is totally wrong in the fullest sense of the word. But please understand, when he admitted that even only this one thing is wrong, he gave away the game. Regardless of whether he or anyone else would own up to it, the perception of "wrongness" has to come from somewhere. There must be a source for the software.

Subjectivity: The Argument That Doesn't Hold Water

Many people believe in the notion of moral subjectivism. That means there *are* no universally binding moral obligations. (By contrast, moral objectivism says there are universal morals and absolutes. This is what the Bible teaches.) Nevertheless, moral subjectivism admits there is a conscience. In fact, it dictates that people have to determine what is right or wrong specifically by listening to their consciences.

The rule of subjectivism says, "If there is really a guideline you should follow, it is this: never disobey your conscience." Interestingly, though, the direction never to disobey is an absolute statement, and it raises a fascinating question. If our conscience is so significant that it should be the supreme determinant of what we should and shouldn't do, then where did the conscience get such monarchical authority? In answering the question, philosophers and thinkers on all sides of the debate have determined there are only four possible sources for this authority.

Nature

The authority of our consciences could have come from natural processes. In the evolutionary scheme of things, this would be the realm of animal instinct and survivability of species. The odd thing about this line of argument is that it suggests this great guiding authority came into being from something less great than we are. Animal instincts aren't much of a mentor. Animals readily kill each other for food. Even within species, the more dominant ones often keep food for themselves rather than sharing. Nature is a cruel teacher. So is that really where we get our values? Nature, we can see, has no moral authority.

Ourselves

Some people say we get our consciences from within ourselves. We develop our own guidance system. Here, though, we can point at scores of individuals who followed their own direction and have been quite thoroughly evil. Hitler, Osama bin Laden, and Saddam Hussein decided they were right, but people know intuitively that they were wrong. Few people have ever argued seriously that the Holocaust of World War II or flying passenger planes into office buildings are good things. These were evil people. However, if we conclude that each man or woman legitimately creates his or her own standard of morality, this leads to the possibility that it is OK for each person to do whatever horrible things he or she thinks best.

Another problem is that rules we each set for ourselves simply aren't binding, no matter how loudly we proclaim them. Imposing your own values on yourself is like locking yourself in a room, insisting you can't get out, but keeping the key in your pocket. In reality, you can let yourself out anytime you want. Whenever sufficient temptation comes along to convince you to break the rules, you're "outta there."

Some would say the conscience is instinct, but instinct refers to drives that attract us to or repel us from something. The conscience is different because it is moral *thought*, knowledge independent of our feelings. Many times conscience will override instinctual feelings or desires. On occasions, we may want to do something, but conscience tells us not to obey our instincts.

Society

If the conscience does not come from less than me (nature) and if it does not come from me (the individual), many people contend it comes from others like me, others equal to me. That is what we call society—simply more people, a collection of human beings.

But let's think about this for a minute. Can quantity really produce an absolute? Can 1 million people vote and bring about a moral truth? Although there are no perfect societies, we can point to plenty of bad ones. There have been cannibalistic people and societies that sacrificed babies. So more of a bad thing doesn't at some point become a good thing. If we pile yet another truckload on a dung heap, it will never become chocolate ice cream. Society is more of the same, not a higher power.

God

So if conscience does not come from something less than me, from me, or from others like me, then it must come from something beyond any of these things—from something higher or superior to me. But what could qualify as something greater than I? That would have to be a moral God.

Morality is a spiritual thing because there is no correlation between morals and molecules, between inner direction and matter. Only the "God position" can explain the over-arching authority of the conscience. Keep in mind that we've proposed these four ideas in answer to the question raised by moral subjectivism: the directive that the highest good is to follow one's own conscience. The Bible doesn't promote subjectivism. It teaches that there is an objective moral code. The point is that *even if* we reject objectivism and embrace subjectivism (the only two philosophical possibilities), we still end up at the same place: God is the only possible source of the conscience.

Treasure in the Soil of Your Soul

If you were digging in a field and found a bag of gold, one question you would *not* ask is: "Did somebody put that there?" You would know someone buried the treasure. It's an automatic—and completely reasonable—assumption. If you wondered anything, it would be, rather, "*Who* buried the gold?"

The conscience is the treasure God buried in our souls. If anyone admits the existence of the conscience, it makes the existence of God extremely high on the scale of probability. To use our courtroom method, we're moving beyond any reasonable doubt that God exists. That's based simply on the logical process through which we've explored the idea so far. Now, though, I'd like to take us a step further and show why the conscience suggests that not just any sort of God exists but why the specific God revealed in the Bible is the only One who can account for the conscience as we know it.

Friedrich Nietzsche, a famous atheist, explained: "If God does not exist, then everything is permitted." Nietzsche, who proclaimed that God is dead, preached this viewpoint. He understood that the "death of God" meant the destruction of all meaning and value in life. If there is no God, there is no real right or wrong—no rules, no such thing as sin.

Here is a part of the equation that atheists don't consider. Their logic points in a very revealing direction. It is valid to say that because there is no God, there is no morality. No God = no morality. That is true.

But what about the reverse of the statement? If there is morality, then there is a God. The logic follows, and we have observed that morality—as exhibited by the conscience—does exist. So I will say it this way: since morality exists, God exists. And the type of morality we experience through the conscience reflects the nature of the God of Scripture. Likewise, sin is what it is because God is who he is. Without any standards, we have violated nothing, but with standards based in the character of an all-powerful God, there *are* standards, and honoring them matters very much indeed. Conscience—what Romans 2:15 calls the law written on our hearts—is the voice of God in our lives, telling us what matters.

Installed for a Purpose

The Bible explains that the conscience has a twofold purpose.

First, it affirms when we do well. The conscience directs us toward righteous things. Whenever we do something good, we feel good inside. Even if we do something upright and no one else knows about it, we are still rewarded with a special feeling in our hearts. That's the inner software designed to encourage us to be the kind of person a God of character wants us to be.

On the other hand the conscience also accuses. It will punish us. If we do something wrong, we hear the alarms go off as we move out of the cone of silence. And as with an aircraft that ignores the warnings and stays outside the cone, serious damage can result. The first step toward destruction is that the warning system begins to overheat. It malfunctions. The Bible points out in 1 Timothy 4:2 that some people's "consciences are seared." When you burn your tongue on hot liquid, the next bite of food has no taste. Burn your tongue enough, and the searing will assure that your taste buds will never again function properly. You won't ever taste another steak.

Wake Up and Smell the Garbage

A damaged—seared—conscience is like living in garbage. Andrei Schwartz directed a television documentary called *Wasteland*, a fascinating account of people who actually live and work in a garbage dump. These destitute individuals scrounge day after day and night after night for a meager subsistence. Twenty-four hours a day, they're in the junkyard. Longtimers even get mad when others move into the dump because competition for the good scraps of food and usable pieces of stuff increases. They get jealous over the garbage!

The makers of the dump documentary found the odor of the place repugnant, but they realized it didn't bother the residents at all. Apparently, once they got used to living in the dump, they didn't notice the stench. But what is the danger of becoming immune to the smell of putrid surroundings? Eventually, we cease to realize the danger—from disease, malnutrition, infection, violence—of the situation. The alarm system no longer works.

Garbage disposal is a challenge for any society but nowhere more than in the United States. Here, we generate enough trash to fill up one hundred thousand garbage trucks *every day*. In one day, we toss out fifteen thousand tons of packing material. Every year, we throw away *75 billion* aluminum cans. Each day, Americans dispose of twenty thousand cars and four thousand trucks. We dump 14 billion tons of trash into the ocean annually. And we throw away 273 million tires—3.6 million tons—every twelve months.

We're also cluttering space with garbage. Thousands of nuts, bolts, gloves, and other "mission debris" form an orbiting garbage dump around the earth. And this garbage is deadly. A 1999 study showed that 4 million pounds of space junk were in low orbit around the earth, traveling seventeen thousand miles per hour—110,000 objects large enough to damage a satellite or a space-based telescope. A speck of paint from a satellite, for instance, once slammed a hole nearly a quarter-inch wide into a space shuttle window. Garbage is dangerous!

The point in talking about garbage is that we should stay away from it. We're supposed to be repelled by the smell, not want to live in it, if we want to be healthy. Our consciences, likewise, alert us to the smell of moral "garbage" that often seems to be all around us. People produce tremendous amounts of moral refuse, and it is the job of conscience to keep us out of it. This is important both now and in the very long run—for eternity.

Ignoring the Light

On December 29, 1972, an Eastern Airlines flight took off from New York, headed for Miami. A book and two movies were made several years later about why that airplane never arrived at the Florida city. Its spectacular crash on approaching the airport fascinated investigators and the public alike because there was absolutely nothing significantly wrong with the airplane, yet it smashed to the ground, killing all on board in perfect weather. How did it happen?

Shortly before landing, the flight crew noticed the light that indicates the landing gear is down did not come on, but the wheels were, in fact, in place just as they should be. The problem was not the landing gear but a burned-out light bulb on the instrument panel. The pilot, copilot, and engineer all recognized the bulb as the real problem but became so preoccupied with fixing the light they forgot to fly the plane. The copilot, who was supposed to be handling the touchdown, stomped and pounded on the panel and didn't pay attention to instructions from air traffic control. Because of ignoring directions from the tower, the plane crashed and more than one hundred people lost their lives.

A lot of people live their lives like that and risk personal disaster. God has placed a mechanism inside each of us through which he gives instructions about how to live a healthy life. The conscience is God's air traffic control through which he offers to communicate with us, sounding the alert when we veer to the left or the right or congratulating us when we don't. God wants to keep each of us in the cone of silence. We best pay attention, especially now that we know he's the source.

CHAPTER THREE

The Uncommonly Common Consent

Prosecutor: *You are the chair of historic and religious studies and professor of world history at UCLA, are you not?*

Expert Witness: *Yes, that is correct.*

Prosecutor: *Are you familiar with a philosophical concept called the argument from common consent?*

Witness: *Yes again. The argument claims that throughout history the majority of the world's population has maintained a belief in the existence of God.*

Prosecutor: *Do you believe the argument is based on a correct assumption?*

Witness: *No, I do not. Aside from a multiplicity of vastly different religious systems, a long history of atrocities is very problematic to believing God exists.*

Prosecutor: *What sort of atrocities?*

Witness: *Unconscionable happenings such as the Crusades, the Inquisition, and the Salem witch trials, to name a few. During the Crusades, defenseless communities were slaughtered—including the elderly, babies, and pregnant women. In the Inquisition, the church tortured "heretics" to death. Here in America, the Salem witch trials saw twenty people condemned as witches by religious paranoia. A belief in God—especially Christianity—has played a key role in some of the greatest horrors in human history. For many people, this has created an insurmountable roadblock to faith and provides compelling evidence* *against the concept of God.*

Defense Attorney: *Professor, is it your opinion that Christian motives were behind the events you just cited?*

Witness: *If you're asking if I believe these crimes are congruent with the Christian faith, the answer is no.*

Defense: *Then since you recognize a clear difference between the teachings of Christianity and these atrocities, isn't it possible—perhaps even likely—that many perpetrators of these events were not Christians at all?*

Witness: *Yes, that's possible.*

Defense: *Are you familiar with Increase Mather?*

Witness: *He was a Puritan leader during the time of the Salem witch trials.*

Defense: *That's correct. And what was the Cases of Conscience Concerning Evil Spirits?*

Witness: *It was a treatise Mather wrote on the fallacy of spectral evidence for convicting witches.*

Defense: *A treatise that was pivotal in putting an end to the witch trials?*

Witness: *Yes.*

Defense: *You're reporting, then, that a Christian was responsible for stopping the witch trials. Professor, let me put the shoe on the other foot for a moment and ask this question: Did you know that, according to Courtois's* Black Book of Communism,[1] *an estimated 100 million people have died under Communist rule during the twentieth century?*

Witness: *No. I have not read that particular book.*

Defense: *Who is the founder of communism?*

Witness: *Karl Marx.*

Defense: *Was he a Christian?*

Witness: *No, certainly not. He was an atheist.*

Defense: *So, what do pogroms and other atrocities necessarily have to do with belief in God? Do they point to no God or to aberrant human behavior?*

Witness: *Well, clearly behavior is an issue.*

Defense: *Apparently, both sides appear to be guilty at times, but your line of reasoning doesn't actually address the historical argument from common consent, does it? So now, speaking strictly as a historian reporting*

31

the facts about the original concept we discussed, would you believe most
people and cultures throughout history have believed in some sort of deity?
Witness: *Yes. Without question.*
Defense: *Then it would seem the common consent that God exists is not*
so terribly uncommon.

Sometimes when I am out in public, people take an extra long look at the clothes I'm wearing, and I think, "Uh-oh. I've done it again." They probably wonder what country I'm from because they observe a serious defect in the color combinations exhibited by my wardrobe selections. But I'm actually not as fashion challenged as they think. The truth is I am color blind. If my color combination is gruesome, I can't tell. That's why I check out my fashions with my wife every day before I leave the house.

I have known I am color blind since I was a senior in high school. That's when I first took the Ishihara test for color blindness. This test presents a series of colored circles within which are printed other color spots in the shape of numbers. If someone can see the numbers, he's normal. If not, he's color blind.

Because color blindness is a genetic trait, I recently wondered if anyone else in my family is color blind, so I gave the Ishihara test to my wife and four children. It turns out that if *they* pick poor combinations of clothing, it's because they are, in fact, fashion challenged. Happily, I found that none of them are color blind. Everyone in my family can see the Ishihara numbers but me. If, based on our individual observations, the family had voted on whether or not the numbers exist on the pages of the test, it would have been four to one in favor of their existence.

Now if we voted, I could argue with them, trying to convince my wife and kids that those numbers do not exist, but it would be pointless. They are convinced the numbers are there. It is virtually impossible for a color blind person like me to convince a normal person that my view of color is true. I am the abnormal minority.

The Blind Few

Color blindness occurs in about 5 percent of the American male population. But it is fascinating to note that men cannot pass on this condition to their sons. Neither of my boys are color blind, and that's because my *wife* is not color blind. While boys can have this condition if just the mom carries the color-blindness gene, in order for a girl to be color blind she has to have both a mother who is a carrier and a father who is color blind. As a result, color blindness occurs in females in only 0.64 percent of the American population. However, the stats can be different elsewhere.

In 1997, zoologist Oliver Sacks wrote a book titled *The Island of the Color Blind.* He tells the story of the Island of Pingelap in Micronesia. On this small island, one in twenty people is afflicted with not just standard color blindness—inability to see true color—but with *monochromatic* color blindness. They see *only* black and white. By contrast, monochromatic color blindness affects only one in *forty thousand* people in the American population. So how did this come to be?

In 1775, a typhoon hit the island, killing all but twenty people who lived there. This hardy remnant went on to repopulate the island, but one of the men was afflicted with monochromatic color blindness. His genetic contribution to such a restricted population assured a far higher than usual incidence of monochromatic color blindness from then on.

The Minority Retort

By some quirk, the proportion of people in our population who claim to be atheists is about the same as people who are color blind. Both represent about 6 percent of the populace. Whatever the reason for this similarly sized chunk of people, it does provide an in-teresting analogy. Let me explain.

Historically, most Americans believe in God. Since 1947, the Gallup Poll has tracked the number of Americans who say they believe in God, and here's how we stack up:

- 1947: 94 percent claimed to believe in God (6 percent didn't)
- 1953: 98 percent (2 percent didn't)
- 1967: 98 percent (2 percent didn't)
- 1975: 94 percent (6 percent didn't)
- 1996: 96 percent (4 percent didn't)[2]

As with color blindness, then, the obvious question is to wonder who actually is blind—the minority or the majority. That thought is central to the common consent argument about God.

Common consent suggests it is reasonable to deduce that some sort of divine being exists simply because the overwhelming majority of people who have ever lived have taken the idea seriously. The Bible also explains how completely ubiquitous this reality is. Romans 1:18–20 declares: "For God's wrath is revealed from heaven against all godlessness and unrighteousness of people who by their unrighteousness suppress the truth, since what can be known about God is evident among them, because God has shown it to them. From the creation of the world His invisible attributes, that is, His eternal power and divine nature, have been clearly seen, being understood through what He has made. As a result, people are without excuse." The Bible says God is so clearly seen that every single person who has ever lived in any period of history is without excuse if he or she thinks God isn't real.

Primitive Consent

A simple way to phrase the argument from common consent is, "Everyone knows there is a God." We've talked about it so far from the standpoint of common logic (can so many people all be wrong?). Theologians, too, have addressed this issue and call their version the argument from universal consent. Since every single culture in human history has be-lieved in an ultimate reality, it is as though people are hardwired to think that God is.

Missionaries have noted that when they meet non-Christian tribes in remote areas, they do not discover atheists. Rather, they find people who believe in a god, and often in many gods. These people fear judgment after death, and they're worried about the con-sequences of the things they do wrong.

Profound Consent

Throughout history, even great minds have believed in God—most notably great scientists. As the scientific revolution of the Renaissance took shape, the breakthroughs that led to what we now call modern science were made by men who also were devout believers in God. Here are a few:

· *Nicolaus Copernicus* (1473–1543), the Polish astronomer who put forth the first mathematical system of planets going around the sun. He often referred to God in his writings.

· *Johannes Kepler* (1571–1630), a brilliant mathematician and astronomer and a devout Christian, established the laws of planetary motion around the sun.

· *Galileo Galilei* (1564–1642) perfected the telescope and determined that the sun, rather than the earth, is the center of our solar system. Although the Roman Catholic Church at the time condemned his views, Galileo argued his system had no problem because he started with the assumption that the Bible does not err, and he was simply putting forth his system as a way to interpret the Bible. (By the way, in 1992, Pope John Paul II agreed that the Roman Catholic Church had made a mistake in condemning Galileo.)

· *René Descartes* (1596–1650), French mathematician, scientist, and philosopher, is called the father of modern philosophy. A devout Christian, he was a key figure in the development of the scientific method.

· *Sir Isaac Newton* (1642–1727), an undisputed figure of genius and innovation, is known for mechanics and mathematics. Newton saw mathematics as central to all science, and he shares the honor of inventing calculus. Regarding the origin of the universe, Newton observed, "The most beautiful system of the sun, planets, and comets could only proceed from the counsel and dominion of an intelligent and powerful being."[3]

· *Francis Bacon* (1561–1626) was a believer and an English philosopher, essayist, jurist, and statesman. Most notably, he was lord chancellor of Parliament. Bacon helped develop the scientific method of solving problems.

· *Blaise Pascal* (1623–62), a brilliant scientist and mathematician, became a devout Christian at the age of thirty-one as a result of his logical inquiry into the question of God. (Chapter 10 of this book focuses primarily on a stirring argument for God developed solely by Pascal and known as Pascal's wager.)

· *Robert Boyle* (1627–91), founder of the Royal Society in London and considered the father of modern chemistry, was a man of deep theological conviction.

· *Michael Faraday* (1791–1867), the son of a blacksmith and a committed Christian, became one of the greatest scientists of the nineteenth century. His book on electricity and magnetism revolutionized physics.

- *Gregor Mendel* (1822–84), a Catholic monk, laid the mathematical foundations of genetics. Recognized as a devout believer, he was elected the abbot of his monastery in 1868.

- *Louis Pasteur* (1822–95), a strong believer, searched for evidence of spontaneous generation for twenty years but never found it. The quest led to his discovery of the law of biogenesis, that only life begets life.

- *Kelvin William Thompson* (1824–1907). Lord Kelvin was a British scientist and a Christian who laid the foundation for modern physics. Because of his numerous earned and honorary degrees from European universities, he was said to have had more letters after his name than anyone else in the British Commonwealth.

- *Max Planck* (1858–1947) made many contributions to physics but is best known for his work on quantum theory, which revolutionized our understanding of the atomic and subatomic world. He was a church warden from 1920 until his death.

- *Albert Einstein* (1879–1955) was likely the best known and most highly regarded scientist of the twentieth century. He is responsible for stunning leaps ahead in our understanding of time, gravity, and matter (think: E = MC2). Although he never committed to a personal belief in God, Einstein recognized the impossibility of a noncreated universe. He once said, "I want to know how God created the world. I want to know His thoughts. The rest are details." [4]

This list could go on, but the point is that an overwhelming number of the world's greatest thinkers in science, mathematics, and philosophy have believed in God.

In God We Trust

Belief in God is true not only of many great thinkers but also of many great governments. Most have held to some sort of belief in a supreme being. In modern times, there is no better example than the United States of America. The United States was founded as "one nation under God," and God is referenced thoroughly in things American. He's mentioned in the Declaration of Independence ("We hold these truths to be self-evident, that all men are created equal, that they are endowed by their *Creator* with certain unalienable rights, that among these are life, liberty, and the pursuit of happiness"), the Pledge of Allegiance ("one nation under *God*"), and on our money ("In *God* we trust").

Not only that, God is invoked in forty-seven of our fifty state constitutions, and no U.S. president has ever claimed to be an atheist. Virtually every president since Washington has talked about God in his public speaking and often in inaugural addresses.

The first Congress began with a prayer for God's help—a tradition that continues to the present—and it regularly called the nation and state assemblies to prayer. The Founders clearly credited God with forming this nation.

The historical support for the argument from common consent is unequivocal. The vast majority of people in every era have believed in God. But have they all simply been deluded?

What Causes Color Blindness?

In 1794, the English chemist John Dalton published the first scientific paper on color blindness, called "*The Extraordinary Facts Relating to the Vision of Colors.*" With Dalton's paper, the study of color blindness was off and running, and today our knowledge of the condition is astounding. Color blindness, by definition, is the inability of a person to perceive differences between colors that other people—the majority—can distinguish.

We now know that, strangely enough, every person is born color blind. A baby cannot see colors until about four months of age. That is when the cones—the eye's color receptors—begin to develop. (The failure of a youngster's cones to develop is what causes the one-in-forty thousand cases of rod-monochromatic color blindness we mentioned earlier.) Rods are the black-and-white receptors in the eye that monitor darkness and light. Rods and cones make up the retina, a neuromembrane that lines the back of the eye. The human eye is able to see color whenever light stimulates the retina.

If someone has a defect in color vision, one of two things has happened. He might have acquired color blindness, which is extremely rare, and developed the condition at some point in life. The vast majority of color-blind people, however, have inherited their color blindness.

The color we see depends on the sensitivity and range of the pigments in our cones. The reason I cannot see the numbers in the Ishihara test is because something is wrong with the pigments in my cones. The genetic explanation for why I am color blind is that one healthy gene is necessary for someone to see color normally. The problem was passed to me through the X chromosome. Like all boys, I have only one X chromosome, and the gene on that one for me causes color blindness. Because of one affected gene on the X chromosome, more boys than girls are color blind.

The Deluded Majority?

A color-blind person could, of course, *deny* the existence of color. He could claim that those who see color correctly are actually deluded and that the world's true palette is the one that color-blind people see. To draw one more analogy: A tone-deaf person who does not believe in the existence of music could try to talk others out of the idea that beautiful music exists, but a tone-deaf person will never talk a musician out of believing music exists because it is actually the tone-deaf person who is deluded about music.

There have been notable exceptions to the vast number of people who have believed in God. The renowned psychologist Sigmund Freud (1856–1939), for instance, addressed the existence of God in his theories of psychiatry and psychology. He believed people simply made up the concept of God to pacify their own weaknesses. Mankind, he contended, is afraid of the forces of nature and so has to find a way to mollify this fear. Freud claimed that people project their idea of "father" into a false notion they call "God" as a way of making themselves feel secure.

Now think about this. Is God really crafted in our minds in the image of our fathers, or is the reverse true? If all the people who ever believed in God are this deluded, the level of fantasy supercedes by many magnitudes any other collective error in human history! Is this really likely? There is no other subject about which so many people have been wrong time after time in every part of the globe through all the epochs of human history. This level of delusion is simply not tenable.

No One Can See without Light

When a person sees something, he or she actually is perceiving light bouncing off the object and entering the eye. So the presence of light is absolutely crucial to the act of seeing. We cannot visually perceive anything without light. In order to see, we must have two things—a healthy eye and light.

Although light is available in abundance, not all people have healthy eyes, but there is a part of the eye that can be transplanted and restore sight if it happens to be "broken." The cornea is the clear window in front of the eye that allows light to enter. It helps in two ways. The cornea shields the rest of the eye from germs, dust, and other debris and matter, and it is the outermost lens for the eye, crucial for maintaining sharp focus on objects we see. Since the cornea is responsible for 65 to 75 percent of the eye's focusing power, without a healthy one, the eye will never take a clear picture.

Fortunately for people with damaged corneas, they can be replaced. The first successful cornea transplant was done in 1905, and nowadays, this corneal surgery is the most successful of all transplants. The procedure boasts a 90 to 95 percent success rate, and it usually restores vision completely. But there is something startling about a cornea transplant. In order for a person to have the procedure, someone else—the donor—has to die.

Throughout this chapter, we've used color blindness as a metaphor for spiritual blindness, and as with a cornea that doesn't function properly, there is a donor available to restore spiritual sight. The mission of Jesus was to give sight to the blind. His purpose statement is found in Luke 4:18b: "to proclaim freedom to the captives and recovery of sight to the blind."

I Was Spiritually Blind

There was a time in my life that I not only was color blind; I also was blind spiritually. Fortunately, I received a spiritual transplant. God opened my eyes, and now I know Jesus is the light of the world because he has illuminated my life. I believe he is real not just because others have said so but because I have experienced him myself. Now no one can ever talk me out of it. At first, though, I had to pay attention to people who already had sight.

So the fact remains, I have never seen Dr. Ishihara's numbers, bu

I believe they are there. Why? Because countless other people have seen them. That particular blindness is mine, not theirs. Similarly, it's not the billions who have believed in a deity that are wrong.

Speaking of billions, the next argument for God has *hundreds* of billions of witnesses. We call them stars.

CHAPTER FOUR

Cosmology – The Evidence "Out There"

Defense Attorney: *As a professor in the Department of Astronomy and Astrophysics at the University of Chicago and as the director of the Yerkes Observatory, your job in a nutshell is to observe the universe. Would that be a fair assessment?*

Expert Witness: *In a simplistic sort of way, yes. I'd say that's true.*

Defense: *And for the past fifteen years you've been gazing into the heavens and recording your findings.*

Witness: *That's correct.*

Defense: *Do you believe in God, Professor?*

Witness: *Yes, I do. But I haven't always believed he exists. Until about two years ago, I was a confirmed atheist and proponent of naturalistic evolution.*

Defense: *So you've been in your field fifteen years, and two years ago you revamped your thinking about God. That's thirteen years of your career that you did not believe in God. What changed your mind?*

Witness: *A desire for intellectual honesty. From childhood, my father taught me Darwinian evolution—that man descended from a common ancestor with apes, that our thoughts, dreams, and desires are nothing more than random neurosynaptic firings, that life emerged from the primordial ooze. Every scientific textbook I read in school and all of my science teachers said the same thing: "Life has no inherent meaning. Everything in our universe came from nothing. There is no God!" But when I gazed through the telescope into the night sky, what I saw continually screamed at me to the contrary.*

Defense: *Like what?*

Witness: *Like our own world, for instance, and its placement in the universe. The earth's axis is tilted at a twenty-three-degree angle, precisely the right slant to allow even distribution of the sun's rays. Alter it just one degree in either direction, and the food chain would cease to exist. And consider: Of the nine planets in our solar system, Earth is the only one that has exactly the right gases and mixtures to give us the air we breathe.[1] Also, the earth is positioned 93 million miles from the sun, hurtling along its path at nearly 65,000 miles an hour, and spinning as it goes at more than 1,000 miles per hour. If our orbit were slowed by a third or the rotation rate reduced by even one-tenth, all life on this planet would be incinerated! [2]*

Defense: *So what are you telling us, Professor?*

Witness: *I believe it's impossible to examine honestly and thoroughly the order and precision of the heavens and then rationally conclude there is no God. Randomness couldn't have brought this about. A Designer and Creator had to set up the cosmos.*

Prosecutor: *So you suggest that you're being honest while thousands of other scientists are not? Isn't it possible, Professor, that you're the one who's misinterpreting the data? Are you maintaining that throughout your illustrious career you have never been wrong?*

Witness: *That was not my point.*

Prosecutor: *Have you ever been wrong?*

Witness: *Yes, of course I have.*

Prosecutor: *I see. I'm glad you can acknowledge that. Thank you so much, Doctor, for your intellectual honesty.*

Defense: *Professor, what was it you were wrong about?*

Witness: *The theory of evolution. I was wrong about the theory of evolution and the idea that everything came about by chance.*

Defense: *Yes, Doctor. Thank you again for your intellectual honesty.*

A relatively small part of America boasts a remarkable array of impressive statistics. Covering about forty-seven square miles, it is roughly the size of San Francisco. This spot is the largest single-site employer in the United States with as many as sixty thousand workers on location at some times. Guests at this place consume more than 50 million soft drinks each year, as well as 10 million hamburgers, 7 million hot dogs, 9 million pounds of french fries, and more than 150 tons of popcorn. Since 1971, the miles logged by its trains would equal more than thirty round-trips to the moon, and it is the home of the two highest mountains in the state of Florida—Thunder Mountain at 197 feet above sea level and Space Mountain, 180 feet tall. If someone wanted to stay in every hotel and guest room offered there and stayed only one night in each, it would take him seventy-two years to lodge in all the rooms. I am referring, of course, to Disney World. Perhaps it is not such a "small world after all."

Even though millions of people visit Disney World each year, there is one thing every visitor—man, woman, child, old, young—has in common. Regardless of what country these people are from (and there are many), what philosophical or religious beliefs they hold, or what mode of transportation they used to get to the spot, there is one thing they all assume, even if they've never given it a conscious thought. Every visitor to Disney World believes that someone or some group of people designed and built the place. No one who goes there assumes the whole thing was an accident. No one thinks Disney World just happened.

When people visit this amazing place, it is crystal clear they are participating in a gigantic planned community. It was created for the enjoyment of its visitors, and it reveals astounding ingenuity and imagination. There is also this astonishing faith on the part of all Disney World guests that someone made it. Yet, no one today knows the person who started it all. Walt Disney, the man whose brilliance gave rise to the Disney enterprise, is long deceased. And few Disney customers have met the visionaries who followed and implemented Mr. Disney's dreams, but all believe the makers are there somewhere. And why not? There is nothing in our experience of life that suggests a wondrous place as complex and entertaining as Disney World happened by chance. Strangely, though, many people take exactly that attitude toward an even more remarkable place we all live in every day.

The cosmos—our world—is still a more mind-boggling arrangement than the Disney setup. It would make sense, then, to assume someone behind this universe, like Florida's otherworldly resort, made it the way it is. Yet many people fail—or choose not—to recognize that obvious fact.

Stretching the Limits

Psalm 19:1 says, "The heavens declare the glory of God, and the sky proclaims the work of His hands." The Bible teaches clearly that the universe was designed and created by an all-powerful, all-intelligent being called God. Scripture offers convincing evidence that the universe is not an accident, and it is fascinating to see how modern science discovers little by little how accurate the ancient document actually is.

Seventeen verses in the Bible state explicitly that God has expanded the universe from its original size, a fact science has confirmed. Of this expanding universe, Isaiah artfully explains that God "created the heavens and stretched them out" (42:5a) and "He stretches out the heavens like thin cloth and spreads them out like a tent to live in" (40:22b; see other similar verses in Isa. 44:24b; 45:12b; 48:13a; and 51:13a). The prophet Jeremiah recorded the same ideas. Jeremiah 51:15 notes, "He made the earth by His power, established the world by His wisdom, and spread out the heavens by His understanding." Job, likely the oldest book in the Bible, concurs: "He alone stretches out the heavens" (9:8a). Other Scriptures have similar testimonies:

- Psalm 104:2: "He wraps Himself in light as if it were a robe, spreading out the sky like a canopy."
- Zechariah 12:1b: "The Lord, who stretched out the heavens, laid the foundation of the earth."

The first of these biblical observations was made about 2000 BC, and the last one was recorded around 500 BC.

The Big Bang

The famed astronomer Edwin Hubble confirmed these ancient references in 1927 when he found stunning evidence that the universe has been expanding. This concept of expansion has come to be known as the big bang theory and is based on the notion that some sort of explosive action caused the massive expansion of the universe—hence the name big bang.

Since many people ask me if I believe in the big bang, let me state clearly that I do not believe in a *naturalistic* big bang that did not originate from the action of a divine being. Many hold that the big bang was not the result of God but was a huge explosion in the universe that merely happened. I would argue, though, that a big bang without a big God is nothing but an explosion. And explosions always create chaos, not order.

An Orderly Explosion?

The universe is a marvel of orderliness, and again, I point out that our everyday world is the foundation from which we extrapolate information about those things we can't see. It is logical to do this—to reason from what we see and know to discern things we do not see and want to discover.

Here's the basic observation from which we can string our line of reasoning: if a bomb goes off, it does not produce order. In fact, the general purpose of an explosion is to create disorder. We blow things up to destroy them, not to create them. And no matter how long we wait after the explosion goes off, order will not come about. Berlin, Hiroshima, and Nagasaki would still be rubble today if after World War II we had simply waited around to see if the cities would come back into being on their own.

No, explosions create destruction and chaos, but when we look at the cosmos, we see a marvel of orderliness. In our solar system, three planets—Venus, Uranus, and Pluto—rotate in the opposite direction from the other six planets. Even if an explosion somehow set the planets into being, the physics of the situation dictate that all nine should be spinning in the same direction. So even such a seemingly simple thing as planetary rotation is difficult to explain with an explosion theory. Hubble brilliantly deduced that we live in an "expanded" universe—just as the Bible says—yet the suggestion that it was expanded by a mindless explosion simply doesn't jibe with what we can reasonably deduce.

The Finite World

In addition to the somewhat general suggestions about our universe expanding, the Bible gives us many fascinating facts about the cosmos. For one thing, it teaches that the universe is finite. Quite to the contrary, there have been many scientists in the course of history who have argued that the universe is infinitely old and infinitely wide. Thanks in large part to the discovery of the laws of thermodynamics, however, contemporary science has completely debunked that concept. The *Scientific American* published a paper in April 1999, giving a technical explanation of why scientists now believe the universe must be finite, and it noted that the vast majority of serious cosmologists agree the universe is limited in size and age.[3]

We've already noted that Scripture observes the universe had a beginning—that is to say, the cosmos is not infinitely old. The Bible also assures us the world will have an end. It won't last forever: "All the heavenly bodies will dissolve. The skies will roll up like a scroll" (Isa. 34:4a). And in Revelation 6:14: "The sky separated like a scroll being rolled up; and every mountain and island was moved from its place."

Space, too, in the universe is limited. Psalm 147:4 says, "He counts the number of the stars; He gives names to all of them." God knows the exact number of stars and has even named them. We, too, have done our best to figure how many stars there are. Now we know there are roughly 50 billion galaxies in the universe, each containing several billion stars. The number is big, but it is finite.

Of course, even billions upon billions are merely an estimate. The Bible points out that the specific number of stars cannot be determined. Jeremiah 33:22a says, "The hosts of heaven cannot be counted; the sand of the sea cannot be measured." There are similar references in Genesis and Hebrews. Together, these give us a wide range of observations: Moses wrote Genesis in the fifteenth century BC, Jeremiah wrote in the seventh century BC, and Hebrews was written in the first century AD.

Strangely enough, in all three of these ancient periods, astronomers believed that they had, in fact, numbered all of the stars. The ancients believed there were about three thousand of them. That was the most they could see at any one time. An observation from the Southern Hemisphere might have doubled the number to six thousand, but the point is at the time people thought they knew how many stars the universe contained, the writers of the Bible maintained that the stars are countless. Why? I believe it's reasonable to deduce that the Bible had access to information that a mere human being could not possibly have had. The One who made the stars told his writers of Scripture the way things really are.

Little by little we mere humans have discovered just how correct the biblical writers were. Galileo first used the telescope to observe stars. In 1608, with his expanded vision, he recorded a tenfold increase in the number of stars. He counted about thirty thousand! But, of course, that is not the end of the story. Today, using high-powered telescopes on Earth and in space, our generation of scientists estimates the number of stars at seventy sextillion—70,000 million million million! Here's what that number looks like: 70,000,000,000,000,000,000,000. This is a colossal number of stars. To help us grasp this unfathomable fact: there are about ten times the number of stars in the universe as there are grains of sand on all the beaches and deserts on Earth. So will we ever figure out the exact number? No way.

Finding the Center

Another mystery about our planet and why things are the way they are bears serious consideration. To start again with the Bible, it presents our planet as the most important place in the universe, suggesting even that Earth is the reason everything else was created.

For centuries scientists have debated the role of Earth in the cosmos, some arguing that our planet lies at the center of the universe while some declaring it is not. In 300 BC, Aristotle propounded the idea that the sun is stationary in space with the earth and the planets revolving around it. We get our word *planet* from Greek and Latin—it means "wanderer." Other people thought the stars were fixed and the planets moving. Still others believed the earth was stationary, and the sun moved around us. They thought that if the earth was moving around the sun, it would create immense solar winds. Since they did not observe such winds, they deduced that everything revolves around Earth. This geocentric theory of the universe was popularized in AD 150 by Claudius Ptolemy, who also believed the planets move in circular orbits. This outlook became the official view during the Middle Ages, and its acceptance set the stage for one of history's greatest scientific showdowns.

Copernicus, a Polish astronomer who lived from 1473 to 1543, proposed a radical new theory that the earth moves around the sun, and no less a scientist than Galileo confirmed this heliocentric theory. Because the Bible's contention that the earth is special had come to be associated with the geocentric perspective (even though it is a Greek concept, not specifically Christian), the Inquisition tried Galileo for heresy in 1633. Galileo, in defense, said he did not oppose the Bible in any way—he opposed only Ptolemy. He (rightly) maintained that nothing about the concept of the earth orbiting around the sun is inconsistent with the Bible, even going so far as to declare that when the Bible speaks to science, it is right every time. In his perspective, "The Bible was written to show us how to go to heaven—not how the heavens go."[4]

Further advances in the field of planetary motion were made by Johannes Kepler, a German astronomer and mathematician who lived from 1571 to 1630. He spent twenty-five years studying orbits and confirming the Copernican model. He found, though, that planetary orbits are not circular but elliptical. Kepler's study, in turn, led to a break-through by Sir Isaac Newton, who deduced from Kepler's laws of mechanics a single physical law vital to each and every one of us—the law of gravitation.

Once it was proven that the earth orbits around the sun, this outlook led to speculation that our solar system and galaxy are not at the center of the cosmos either. This theme has become predominant in secular literature, leading popular, atheistic scientists such as the late Carl Sagan to proclaim there is nothing special whatsoever about the earth, that it is here purely by accident. And their contention is not wholly unreasonable if there is nothing unique about the earth's physical location relative to everything else. We wouldn't expect it to be anywhere in particular if the earth merely happened.

The odds of our galaxy being near the center of the universe by accident are less than one out of a trillion. So if we should happen to find out that the universe is *galactocentric* and that our galaxy is the one at the center, the implications are very profound indeed.

Which Came First?

The Bible, in the book of Genesis, reports that God created the earth on day one of six days in which the universe was created. Three days later (day four), he created the sun, the moon, and the stars. The Bible's teaching is crystal clear that the earth was first, and this has implications many people find disturbing. It's troublesome because no matter what model of creation is put forward, based on Scripture, it will be at odds with current science. Whether we believe the earth is young—thousands of years old—or billions of years old, adding more time in an attempt to reconcile the biblical account with modern science will not work. We always get back to the statement in the Bible that the earth was created first. There's no getting around it.

In Genesis 1:14–15, we see that all of the hosts of heaven—the sun, moon, and stars—exist for the benefit of the earth. Because Earth was created first, everything else came after it and was around it. Atheists try to escape this idea by relegating Earth to an insignificant place in the universe. Sagan devoted an entire book to this single idea. He used our location in the cosmos to belittle Earth and, by implication, us: "The Earth is a very small stage in a vast cosmic arena. Our posturing, our imagined self-importance, and the idea that we have a privileged position in the universe are challenged. Our planet is a lonely speck in the great enveloping cosmic dark. In our obscurity in all this vastness, there are no hints that help will come from elsewhere to save us from ourselves." [5]

This was Sagan's way of saying there is no God. Our place in the universe happened by accident, and we are, therefore, fantastically insignificant.

Sagan's thinking is consistent with much of current scientific philosophy. At the heart of big bang cosmology is the assumption of atheism. Astrophysicist J. Richard Gott, in an article specifically devoted to the Copernican principle, presents this very idea: "The Copernican Revolution thought it was a mistake to assume, without sufficient reason, that we occupy a privileged position in the universe. Darwin showed that in terms of origin we are not privileged above other species. Our position around an ordinary star in an ordinary galaxy in an ordinary super cluster continues to look less and less special." [6]

The notion that we do not occupy a special location has become crucial to naturalistic cosmology. The Copernican principle has helped "displace" us because there are only a few possible special places—like the center of something—in which we could be located, but there are innumerable *nonspecial* places. So in a random universe, it is virtually guaranteed that we will be in one of the myriad nonspecial places. The only rational conclusion that can be drawn if we are found to be in a special place is that we were *put there*. So for naturalists, Copernican reality is a relief. The earth is not at the center of the solar system. By rights, though, their relief should already be consumed by worry over how to interpret some stunning newer discoveries.

Finding Home Base

Early in the twentieth century, scientists discovered an astral phenomenon we now call red shift in the light we see from stars. Red shift is a stretching of the radiation wave-length by the object's movement away from the observer. When astronomers first observed red shift in star light, they assumed everything they observed "shifting" was simply stars. Then, in 1927, Edwin Hubble discovered galaxies, and a whole new universe opened up.

Hubble saw that galaxies actually contain individual stars and that these galaxies are very, very far away from us. Not only that, the galaxies are red shifting—moving away from us at extreme velocities. Also, the more distant galaxies are retreating at even faster speeds than the galaxies closer to us. It was this discovery that led to the big bang theory. Something like a massive explosion, it was reasoned, must have started everything moving away from a center point.

But one central, overwhelmingly significant aspect of the red shift observation is consistently downplayed or deliberately over-looked in virtually every contemporary discussion of the subject among naturalists. The observation is this: except for directions obscured by the Milky Way through which we cannot see, astronomers observe an equal number of galaxies moving away from us in all directions. In fact, if they were to diagram the pattern, it would look like concentric circles—a circle of galaxies, then an empty space, then another circle of galaxies—ring after ring moving progressively faster away from...*us*. If red shift occurs in every possible direction we can look from our vantage point, the inescapable conclusion is that our galaxy is at the very center of the universe. Yet, every naturalistic explanation would argue that the odds against such an occurrence are so gargantuan as to be absolutely impossible. But here we are. Sitting in the middle of 50 billion galaxies. The centerpoint.

Some astronomers have proposed an explanation for why—even though it looks like we are in the center—we actually are not in the center. Cosmologists suggest that the big bang was not an explosion in the way we typically think of an explosion. Rather, it is more like the blowing up of a balloon. They picture three-dimensional space as being the surface of a four-dimensional balloon expanding somehow into four spatial dimensions. In this scheme, supposedly no galaxy could claim to be uniquely at the center. True center would be in a region within the balloon, a region that inhabitants on the outside could not perceive.

The problem with the theory is that if we were on the surface of this balloon, it would be reasonable to think we could see into—and through—this center and that we would observe galaxies on the other side of the balloon moving toward us. But that's not what we see. Red shift implies that the universe has a center, and our galaxy is extremely close to it.

Dr. Russell Humphreys, a nuclear physicist, has written extensively on this subject. He pointed out the astounding fact that the technical literature of astronomy almost completely ignores: a galactocentric cosmos is a possible explanation for red-shift quantization. He noted the tendency of astronomers to avoid the obvious and suggested they are doing so because it would call into question their deepest worldview. Humphreys argued that the arrangement of the galaxies moving away in concentric circles with us in the center could not have happened by accident.[7] A galactocentric universe with our galaxy at the center points us right back to the Bible.

Just for You

Just as Disney World was created for its customers, the Bible teaches that the universe—yes, the entire universe—was created for humans. We call this the anthropic principle (derived from the Greek word *anthropos* that means "man"). The layout of the universe implies that it was uniquely created for life and specifically for mankind. This is consistent with what the Bible teaches us—that on day four (Gen. 1:14–19) God made the sun, moon, and stars for the benefit of the people he would make on day six. Why? Because people need these things to divide the day from the night.

Human beings function differently at night than in the daytime. Most sleep at night and work during the day. It is a cycle that seems to have been set up with us in mind.

Of the purpose for sun, moon, and stars, the Bible also says they are to be used for navigation. For centuries, navigators have used constellations to guide ships at sea and to traverse land in remote places.

The Bible points out that the sun, moon, and stars also were set in place for seasons. Rotations and orbits of the earth regulate the seasons as well as days and years. A day is the time it takes for the earth to rotate on its axis (a twenty-four-hour period), and a month is a twenty-nine-and-a-half-day cycle in which the moon orbits the earth. A year is the time it takes the earth to travel around the sun—365 days. All of these are vital time periods for the conduct of human affairs.

Beyond this, another great purpose of the heavens is that they provide light. Without light we would be in big trouble. The Bible says God even gave us a night-light—the moon—besides the one we would expect to have during the day (our sun). We must have light to live.

While it is rational to conclude there is some intention behind the way things work, naturalists have to be content simply to note that the universe is full of amazing *coincidences* that make the whole system work. Consider the moon, for instance. I've already noted its usefulness as a night-light, but it also performs some heroic deeds for us earthlings. It creates the tides that cleanse the oceans and keep our planet from becoming stagnant. To do this, it interacts in just the right way with Earth's gravity, and the gravitational force required to hold the moon in orbit around the earth is incredible. To match its holding power, we would need a steel cable 531 miles in diameter.

Then there are the moon's "signs." One of the most fascinating of all celestial sights is a total eclipse of the sun. Yet this awe-inspiring sight is made possible only because the moon is almost the same angular size in the sky as the sun. To us, it looks about the same size as the sun. The reason is that, while the moon is four hundred times smaller than the sun, it is also four hundred times closer to the earth. We're tempted to think some-one designed it that way so we would know it couldn't have mere-ly happened. And we would be tempted to think that because it is the logical conclusion.

The Alien Autopsy

Although our universe resembles a planned community, it is difficult for naturalists to believe it is planned only for us. To get around that, many scientists have resorted to believing in extraterrestrials. If we were to find extraterrestrial life, then it would be clear the universe was not simply made for man but is home to a Star Wars-like menagerie of life. So crucial is this need to discover extraterrestrial life that, in 1900, the French Academy of Science offered a prize of one hundred thousand francs to the first person who could make contact with an alien civilization.

Nevertheless, in the more than one hundred years since the offer was made, no one has claimed the prize money. Not the barest trace of alien life has been uncovered—and the French Academy is not the only group trying hard to find someone else out there.

SETI stands for the Search for Extraterrestrial Intelligence. The SETI institute has been scanning the skies with the world's most powerful radio telescopes since the 1960s, monitoring thousands of radio frequencies, trying to find extraterrestrial life. Not the barest smidgen of evidence has come forth though.

People ask me all the time if I believe in extraterrestrial life, and I tell them I do not. The many people who do believe, do so without any evidence whatsoever, and I find it amazing that the same people who reject God *in spite of* the evidence might believe in aliens *in the absence* of evidence. Bear in mind, the Bible does not specifically say there is no extraterrestrial life, but there is evidence in Scripture against it.

Maybe It's a BIG World after All

The Bible teaches that the universe was created to sustain us but all for God's glory. Psalm 19:1a says, "The heavens declare the glory of God." The heavens tell of the awesome power and glory of God.

Some skeptics have claimed that the mind-boggling expanse of space is evidence against God. They suggest it doesn't make sense to create a universe so huge. But I submit there is a clear and logical reason why God would do just such a thing: because he wants everyone to know that something *really* big and *really* powerful, *really* awesome and *really* smart created all this stuff we see around us. The bigness itself is not evidence against God—only evidence that we cannot fathom what it would take to create a universe this magnificent. In fact, the bigness speaks of something even bigger that made it.

And how big is this bigness? If we were to ride a beam of light (moving 186,280 miles per second), we could travel from the earth to the moon in two seconds, to the sun in eight minutes, to the edge of the solar system in four months, and to our next closest star in five years. In 100,000 years, we would finally exit our galaxy, but then travel another 1.5 million years before reaching our nearest galactic neighbor. Finally, 4.5 billion years after that, we would arrive at the edge of where we can see with a telescope. Whoever made the universe—far from being denied or derided—deserves a round of applause.

Hidden Clues

The cosmos, as I pointed out earlier, like Disney World, is a planned community. It makes sense to think both worlds have designers. And both designers have left clues to their existence.

Have you ever heard about the hidden Mickeys? Just for the fun of it, the people who built that place hid images of Mickey Mouse throughout the Magic Kingdom. When you go to Disney World, it's a blast to search for hidden Mickeys. I found one in a painting. Another was formed into an image of clouds. But you have to believe they're there, and you have to look very carefully to find them.

The hidden Mickeys have a message for us. They tell us about a winsome designer who wanted to make the world as entertaining as possible. Our cosmos, too, is full of hidden Mickeys. God has left us countless clues that point to a Designer. They support the credible idea of a big God. Galileo found many of these hidden clues, and it helped him grasp also the real message of the Bible—not how the heavens go, but "how to go to heaven." Our conclusion that the clues come from Someone does make sense. So much so, that we need at least one more chapter to grasp fully the significance of all the evidence. Stay with the proceedings.

CHAPTER FIVE

Design Is No Accident

Prosecutor: *The prosecution wishes to enter a book as our exhibit A. Authored in 1859 by Charles Robert Darwin,* The Origin of Species by Means of Natural Selection *is the fundamental basis for evolution— recognized by scientific, educational, political, and religious institutions the world over as the best explanation for life's origin and progression. We also wish to enter several additional books as exhibit B. This collection is but a small group of writings that contain the most current hypotheses and proofs of evolution from men such as Stephen Jay Gould, Douglas J. Futuyma, and Alexander Graham Cairns-Smith. They substantiate the case for Darwinian evolution while they also refute intelligent design.*

Allow me to summarize. Descent with modification, natural selection, and variation are the bases of evolution. Descent with modification means that random natural processes are responsible for creating new species. Natural selection is the inherent struggle for life among all living organisms and the primary force behind evolution. Variation, or mutation, refers to the sporadic hereditary changes that sometimes improve a creature's potential to survive and multiply. It is widely held among the scientific community that these mechanisms, with sufficient time, have the capacity to create complex organisms, and as Futuyma stated in his textbook Evolutionary Biology: *"Darwin made theological or spiritual explanations of the life processes superfluous."*

Now, the defense charges that there are no evolutionary transitions within the fossil record, and, admittedly, we have found few transitional species. However, as scientist Stephen Jay Gould noted, "Paleontolo-

gists have discovered several superb examples of intermediary forms and sequences, more than enough to convince any fair-minded skeptic about the reality of life's physical genealogy."

As you can see then, ladies and gentlemen of the jury, Darwinian evolution—the understanding of origins accepted by the scientific establishment—is a sound, rational system of thought concerning the dawn and development of our universe. It is a system replete with systematic documentation of its claims and well supported by archaeological evidence. The December 31, 1999, issue of Time *magazine added this insightful observation to the discussion: "Charles Darwin didn't want to murder God, as he once put it. But he did."*

Imagine you are walking down a dirt road in the country. Along the way, you're surprised to discover a turtle on top of a five-foot fence post. You can't help but wonder how that shelled animal got there, so you come up with several conjectures. Consider which of these possibilities you would seriously entertain as the explanation:

1. The turtle shinnied up the fence post to get a good view of the countryside.

2. The turtle grabbed a stick and pole-vaulted his way to the top of the fence post.

3. The turtle mutated, growing wings on the back of his shell, and flew to the top of the fence post. Once he landed, he shed the wings, but unfortunately, the turtle let them go too soon because now he is stuck atop the fence post.

4. A mischievous eight-year-old boy found the turtle along the roadside and thought it would be funny to set the creature on the post.

Obviously, number 4 would be your answer. You wouldn't give the others a second thought.

That's the kind of reasonable observation I've been pointing to throughout this book as the basis for our thought processes about God. There are natural, logical patterns of deliberation in which we engage every day that should not be abandoned when we attempt to understand things we cannot perceive with our physical senses. We should assume something is what it seems to be unless we are presented with compelling evidence to the contrary.

If we find an object that appears to have been created for a particular purpose, we should assume our observation is correct unless there's reason to think otherwise. Consider a chair, for example. When we see a chair, we know someone made it, even if we did not see it being made. Why? Because we recognize in the chair an intended purpose: a place for someone to sit down. We realize, too, that in order to have a piece like this, there has to have been a designer who knew how to make a chair fit its intended use.

An Intentional Beginning

Ask someone if she's ever heard the words "In the beginning God created the heavens and the earth," and she'll probably say she has. She'll likely even know that the statement is the opening sentence of the Bible. This most famous of all Bible verses is found, of course, in the book of Genesis. Not surprisingly, the word genesis means "origin" or "beginning," and the Hebrew of Genesis 1:1 is: *bereshith bara Elohim et hashamayim ve'et ha'arets*, a seven-word sentence (to ancient Jews, seven was the number of perfection).

The Bible's opening statement is simple yet deeply profound in its two premises:

1. There is a design to the heavens and the earth.

2. There is a Designer behind the design, and his name is God.

From the very first verse, Scripture throws down the gauntlet in the debate over the fundamental truth of existence. It calls the question and states its position unequivocally. Is there a Being who created the universe or not? And the answer is, yes, and that Being is God. Everyone who has ever lived and ever will live must take one of the two possible positions on the subject: either someone created it all, or he did not.

Many people assert that this universe is not a creation—it merely happened. Because they believe it was a gigantic accident, there is no Designer. What makes the discussion dicey is that both sides—the God and the no-God folks—have to admit the cosmos at least looks as if it has been designed. Our universe reflects stupendous complexity in which nothing seems to be happenstance. The appearance of design is everywhere. There is no random material floating around without purpose; the universe reflects only very intricate design.

The appearance of design in the universe is undeniable. No matter how committed someone may be to atheism, he or she will not convince us that things do not at least seem to be designed. No one could convince us or anyone else of that, which means that the person who chooses to believe that no God designed the universe is left in a very precarious philosophical position. While a theist is free to believe the validity of the observation that everything seems to be designed, the atheist is left only with the awkward assumption that the universe actually exhibits an undesigned design.

Think about that for a minute. What are the logical implications of thinking there could be an undesigned design of some sort? Has anyone ever seen an unpainted painting or an unsculpted sculpture? Has anyone ever lived in an unbuilt house? That's a mind-bending concept—and not only because an elite, intellectually endowed few are capable of grasping the supposed truth of it (although those who maintain the undesigned design position would want us to think our mental capabilities are limited). It's because the idea is simply untenable. It's the emperor's new clothes of philosophy. The idea just doesn't make any more sense than saying there can be dry rain, an elderly newborn, hot ice, or uncooked barbecue (I'm a Texan, and there *isn't* any such thing). We can pick any analogy, but undesigned design is a world-class oxymoron.

Accidental Design?

Charles Darwin popularized the notion of an undesigned design. In 1859, he published *The Origin of Species* in which he postulated that everything—including humans—originated from a single-cell, protozoan-type creature that ultimately evolved into every known life form on earth. The process he described by which all of this happened is his infamous theory of evolution.

Darwin's treatise, though, wasn't the only significant nineteenth-century book on the subject of design. It happens to be the one many scientists flocked to, hoping they could find a reasonable way out of believing in God. William Paley's 1802 work *Natural Theology* made clear that their quest for a sensible alternative came to a far less reasonable conclusion than naturalists would like us to think. In his book, Paley offered a tour of the "museum" of natural theology. He looked at biology, anatomy, physiology, botany, and astronomy, cataloging the enthralling designs we find in every nook and cranny of the natural cosmos.

Paley's accomplishment is all the more stunning when we consider that he did not have access to modern additions to the museum—DNA, genetics, embryology, microbiology. These realms reveal an even more mesmerizing level of design and prove the case even more fully than Paley could have imagined.

Paley developed the famous "watchmaker argument" regarding the origin of the world. He suggested if someone were walking down the road and happened to find a watch, he would not conclude that the watch came into existence as the result of an accident. In fact, he would naturally (and rightly) assume there had to have been a watchmaker who made the timepiece. In *Natural Theology*, Paley explained how the universe is like a giant watch, albeit vastly more complex, which exhibits a design that can point only to a Creator.

As I referenced earlier, that's the position the Bible takes. If we have a creation (and we do), it stands to reason that we have a Creator.

Avoiding the Obvious

Many highly intelligent and creative people have grappled with the question of how the universe could look so designed and yet not have a Designer, and we must give them their due. One such person, zoologist Richard Dawkins wrote a book called *The Blind Watchmaker* in which he contended that although the universe looks like it was designed, it really was not. He noted: "Biology is the study of complicated things that give the appearance of having been designed for a purpose." Dawkins went on to explain that appearance is misleading because it does not reflect design but, instead, natural evolutionary processes that ended up finding a workable reality through random variation and natural selection. His thesis in *The Blind Watchmaker* was that the watchmaker (not God but natural forces) is blind and unconscious.

I offer, though, that the design we see around us is simply too multifaceted and intricate to wave off so lightly. Even Dawkins admitted "that if a complex organ of life is ever found that could not have been formed by numerous, successive slight modifications; I shall cease to believe in Darwinism." Remarkably, he seemed to ignore that his own observations are the undoing of the very position he holds so dear. He explained, for instance, that "each and every plant or animal cell contains a digital-coded database larger in information content than all thirty volumes of the *Encyclopedia Britannica* put together." [1] But get real: undirected material processes do not write encyclopedias, no matter how much time is available.

Simple Complexity?

Early theories on evolution started with the premise that complex organisms evolved from the basic building block of the cell. In the eyes of modern science, this should be immediately recognized as a seriously flawed premise because Charles Darwin and others at this time believed the cell to be a very simple structure. Some diagrams of the cell in Darwin's day show cells to be about as simple as a Ping-Pong ball. With such an understanding, it is more imaginable that a cell could have merely happened. What we now know to be the truth should so seriously debunk that notion as to render it not worth even the most fleeting consideration. Modern biology has revealed a life-giving structure at the cellular level we now say is "irreducibly complex." [2]

Michael Behe has written a book called *Darwin's Black Box* in which he showed how a cell could never have evolved from anything simpler than itself because every facet of its intricate structure is necessary precisely the way it is in order for the cell to function. No part of it could have been anything living until the whole structure combined to function as it does. Behe demonstrated that a cell could never have evolved from gradual steps. It all had to come into being "as is" in order to function. [3]

And that's the mere problem of believing only one individual cell needed to happen into being. What about combining cells into a larger organism?

Your body consists of an estimated 30 trillion cells, and every second of every day, 2 trillion chemical reactions occur in your body that control involuntary functions (such as your heartbeat), disease-fighting functions (white blood cell production), respiratory functions (breathing), and countless other processes beyond the control of the conscious mind. Even as you read this book, you are performing complex feats without thinking about it. You may be fighting a disease you don't even know you have, but do you know why you can do that? It's because your body is programmed to do so.

When you become ill, you expect to get well. You are programmed for health, and you trust your bodily mechanisms to keep you well. When you eat, your digestive system automatically processes the food. Have you ever been bored and decided simply to digest your food for fun? The idea is not even relevant. You couldn't do it even if you wanted to. Digestion does not depend on your intelligence or volition. Even lower animals do it all the time. Dogs are good at digestion. All they have to do is to eat and walk around. Digestion happens because they are designed for it.

We are assembled by an incredible collection of coded information called DNA. So sophisticated is this data system that the DNA of an amoeba can hold the information equivalent of more than one thousand sets of the *Encyclopedia Britannica*. If we took all the DNA out of the 30 trillion cells in the body and stretched them end to end, it would reach to the moon and back half a million times!

The Makings of a Maker

When the Bible says in Psalm 139:14 we are "remarkably and wonderfully made," the clear implication is that we are designed. There is a great story about a group of scientists who believed they had figured out how God made everything, so they went to God with a challenge: "We've figured out how you made everything, and now we believe we can do anything you can. Therefore, we challenge you to a contest to make a man just to show you we can do it too."

God said, "No problem," and offered to go first. So God got some dirt, shaped it, and breathed the breath of life into it—exactly as he did the first time—and again made a perfect man.

The scientists responded simply, "OK, it's our turn now." But as they reached down to get some dirt, God said, "Oh no! You go get your own dirt!"

In the opening line of Genesis, the Hebrew word for God is *Elohim*. But not only is *Elohim* the first word used for God, it is also the most often used word for God in all of Scripture—repeated 2,750 times. It means majesty, honor, and power, and it is this magnificent *Elohim* who created everything.

The word "created"—*barah* in Hebrew—is fascinating too. It means "to create *from nothing.*" And that, as our story about the scientists underscores, is something only an eternal, divine being can do. Anytime you see a *barah* creation in the Bible, it is an act that only God can accomplish. Man cannot create. Only God can bring something into existence from nothing.

A carpenter can make a chair from wood, but a carpenter cannot make a chair from nothing. There is a difference between a craftsman and a creator. The reason mankind cannot make different organisms is we are simply not smart enough, and I believe that is what most galls naturalists.

There is also a difference between creating something and discovering something. Christopher Columbus did not create North America; he discovered it. When we observe our surroundings—these millions of complex species—we discover their fascinating intricacy, but our discovery is not what brings them into being. They were already there thanks to Somebody.

Evolution attempts to explain these things with its three heroes of chance, time, and mutation, but they really are not enough. Darwin anticipated some of the problems with evolution when he stated, "If it can be demonstrated that any complex organ existed which could not possibly have been formed by numerous, successive, slight modifications, my theory would absolutely break down." [4] We've already talked about the complexity of a single cell, and a still more remarkable example troubled Darwin, one through which we see the world.

Seeing Should Be Believing

I believe the greatest example of the inadequacy of Darwin's theory is the eye. Even Darwin admitted he had no explanation for this remarkable organ. The human eye gathers about 80 percent of all the knowledge absorbed by our brains, and it can handle 1.5 million messages simultaneously. To get as much exercise for his or her leg muscles as eye muscles get through normal use, a person would have to walk fifty miles every day, and these same well-toned muscles can make more than one hundred thousand separate motions that direct the eye wherever one wants to look.

Furthermore, the eye contains 130 million light-sensitive rods and cones whose photochemical reactions convert light into electrical pulses that are transmitted to the brain at the rate of

1 billion impulses per *second*. And when confronted with darkness, the eye can increase its ability to see by one hundred thousand times.

If I were a salesman, I would want to sell eyeballs because eyes come fully loaded—automatic aiming, automatic focus, and self-maintenance while one sleeps. What a deal! Eyes are so sophisticated, in fact, that scientists do not fully understand them, and Darwin admitted that the human eye is a stumbling block to evolution: "To suppose that the eye—with all of its inimitable contrivances for adjusting the focus to different distances, for admitting different amounts of light, and for the correction of spherical and chromatic aberration—could have been formed by natural selection seems, I freely confess, absurd. Absurd in the highest degree." [5]

Who's the Original Designer?

Darwin didn't let his misgivings about the human eye stop him though. In attempting to explain how life began, he argued in *The Origin of Species*: "All organisms start from a common origin. From such low and intermediate forms, both animals and plants have been developed. All organic beings, which have ever lived on the earth, may be descended from one primordial form." [6] Everything and everyone—including you and me—trace their heritage back to "one primordial form."

Somehow chance has caused a single-celled organism to grow into every living thing there is. However, neither Darwin nor anyone who has come after him has been able to explain how the single cell came to life. Equally unexplainable is how the cell evolved without any directive intelligence. Naturalists give explanations, of course—supposedly anything can happen given enough time—but all the theorizing amounts to little more than a smokescreen to cover the unalterable fallacy of their position. For instance, supposedly in the distant past, there was green gook. In some fashion, an electrical charge zapped the ooze in just the right way to form a simple protozoan.

Although we've already exposed the myth of a "simple" single cell, even if it were so, what follows is a wishful series of happenings to get to where we are today. The protozoan "complexified" to become a metazoan invertebrate that then evolved into vertebrate fish. Some of these fish developed into amphibians, and these amphibians, in turn, somehow became reptiles. Reptiles grew feathers to become birds, and the birds grew fur and became mammals. A few naturally selected mammals grew into monkeys, and some of these monkeys ended up being people. Despite the passion with which naturalists describe the process, there's really no explanation for the monumental changes, the gargantuan suppositions, and the wholesale shattering of known genetic and physical laws required for the progression to occur.

Besides the difficulty of explaining how the development happened, the idea of evolution also brings up several other unexplainable problems. For instance, what did the first life form eat and how did it reproduce? We also would have to believe life came from nonlife—a process called spontaneous generation that science proved to be impossible about the time Darwin wrote *The Origin of Species*. Finally, we have to accept that intelligence came from nonintelligence—that all the dumb stuff created the smart stuff. Again, it's a supposition contrary to any evidence we've ever seen of how things work.

If It Sounds Impossible, It Probably Is

The truth is evolution has never been observed happening, and no evidence has been found to suggest it ever has happened. Evolutionists theorize it took place slowly, but what the fossil record suggests, rather than gradual evolution, is the instantaneous appearance of life.

The Cambrian fossil layer is the Achilles' heel of evolution. Dr. Daniel Axelrod of the University of California says the Cambrian fossil layer is one of the major unsolved problems of geology and evolution.[7] Even George Gaylord Simpson, known as the crown prince of evolution, noted, "The sudden appearance of life is not only the most puzzling feature of the whole fossil record but its greatest apparent inadequacy." [8]

This has led many evolutionary scientists to come up with a new theory. The late Stephen Jay Gould, a Harvard professor, postulated—along with T. H. Huxley—the theory of punctuated equilibrium.

Punctuated equilibrium declares that the structure of living things remained fairly constant over long periods of time, but then in other, far shorter eras, many species evolved rapidly. When these express phases took place, the evolution was so abrupt and short-lived that there were not enough living transitional forms to leave fossils. Here's how the thinking goes:

· Since fossilization itself is unusual, the sole reason we have any remains at all is that most animals were numerous enough to leave us a record even though only a minute portion of the whole ended up as fossils.

· If there were periods during which very few of any given species were alive, then we shouldn't expect to find remnants of those creatures because it is likely none were ever fossilized.

This conveniently explains what are called "blooms" in the fossil record with no connecting transitional animals, but the question remains whether such a thing should even be construed as evolution. Darwin never suggested the process could happen so quickly. Personally, if I were sitting on the jury, I'd say it sounds a lot more like special creation.

Who Owns the Watch?

On August 2, 1995, the *New York Times* ran a story about a homeless man who became a murder suspect. After a woman was found dead in her apartment, police discovered a digital watch at the crime scene. Investigators were pleased because they knew a person could store numbers and other information in such a watch, and in the memory, they found a rather large number—no other information, only the number. But the number turned out to be a bank code. The police traced it to a bank with several branches in New York City. Although they tried to track down the man whose name was on the account, he was homeless and so had no address (he had been evicted from his house by his mother!). Since police had no other way of finding the suspect, they staked out the banks whose number was in the man's watch. Finally one day the guy activated his code, and the police moved in, arrested him, and had him tried for murder. The fascinating key to this story, though, is that the authorities captured the man because his code was in the watch.

To return to William Paley's analogy, then, we must wonder whose watch we've found when we look at the universe. God's code is the mind-boggling design he's placed everywhere.

A Designer World

In spite of the human eye, regardless of Darwin's admission, and notwithstanding the illogic of undesigned design, we will find few, if any, naturalists who admit to the simple, rational conclusion that the greater the design, the greater the designer. People ask me all the time, "Who made God?" and the answer is: no one. He always was. Naturalists shrug at this point and dismiss the point as an impossibility. Yet I'll maintain as I have throughout this book that our perspective truly draws the more logical conclusion.

A designer great enough to create our universe would be great enough to be eternal. In fact, it must be so. No matter what one's theological position—God or no God—he or she has to face the reality that something somewhere has to be eternal. And it simply makes more sense to say that God is the eternal thing—not the physical universe or series of universes.

The Bible confirms this, of course. Psalm 106:48 explains that God is "from everlasting to everlasting." There never was a time when God was not. The fact that something—anything!—now exists means that something has always existed because we cannot get something—cannot get a design—from nowhere. If something is now alive, it means that something has always been alive. And that Something caused everything. In fact, the idea of cause is such an important point that it is worthy of a chapter all its own. The next one.

CHAPTER SIX

The Effect of a Cause

Prosecutor: *Professor, you hold a PhD in physics and astronomy from the University of Virginia and are the associate professor of biology and chemistry at Columbia University. You've written and lectured for years on the origin of life. Would you give us some background on the subject?*

Expert Witness: *The origins debate centers on two basic premises: (1) That life is the result of undirected, prebiological evolution, or (2) that it is the intentional product of an omnipotent Creator such as the Christian God. I have a hard time swallowing creationism, of course, because the creationist position cannot explain how God created the universe. Prebiological evolution, on the other hand, provides more solid answers.*

Prosecutor: *Would you please explain?*

Witness: *Research in the past century has greatly enhanced Darwin's "primordial broth" concept. The Oparin-Haldane model, for instance, theorizes that Earth's early atmosphere consisted mostly of methane, hydrogen, and ammonia, the organic compounds vital for life. Then in the 1960s, Kenyon proposed that various built-in preferences cause amino acids to link in the proper sequence to create protein molecules, the basis of living cells. More recently, the Cairns-Smith team explained that clay crystals contain qualities from which prebiotic chemicals could assemble. In addition, Sakharov outlined the basic physics regarding the matter/antimatter bias of our universe. Finally, in cosmology the anthropic and multiverse concepts were developed. This allows us to propose that since an infinite number of universes are constantly being formed from nothing, even the most unlikely events must occur. So as you can see, we've* *uncovered some incisive clues in the origins debate.*

Prosecutor: *Thank you, Doctor.*

Defense: *Professor, you cited the Oparin concept that our early atmosphere was composed of ammonia, methane, and hydrogen. Are you aware that in 1980 NASA showed that our atmosphere has never been comprised of those elements but, instead, of nitrogen, water, and carbon dioxide?*

Witness: *I read an article about it at some point. They suggest the composition was similar to what it is today.*

Defense: *And if you were to combine today's atmospheric gases such as carbon dioxide and nitrogen, what would happen?*

Witness: *Well, nothing. They're inert.*

Defense: *Then if the atmosphere was composed of these chemicals, the Oparin-Haldane-Urey concept hardly seems a reasonable scientific evaluation—to base a theory on something we know never was the case. And in Kenyon's work on chemical affinity, researchers selected only ten amino acids for the test. Yet the standard resource, Atlas of Protein Sequence and Structure, lists 250. Did Kenyon pick the proteins at random?*

Witness: *No, the study handpicked them.*

Defense: *Why?*

Witness: *Probably in hopes of producing more favorable results.*

Defense: *Strange. I thought blind chance guided evolution, yet these men deliberately chose ten proteins out of 250 because they knew these ten would produce more favorable results. Others must have wondered about the process, too, because in 1986, a research team decided to test the affinity theory by writing a program that analyzed, not ten, but all 250 proteins. Let me read you a summary of what the team found: "The results demonstrated conclusively that the sequencing had nothing to do with chemical preferences. Consequently, that theory bit the dust. Even Kenyon, one of its biggest proponents, has repudiated the idea." Doctor, you also said Sakharov had unveiled the criteria for understanding the matter verses antimatter bias. Can you give us an example to corroborate his idea?*

Witness: *I'm afraid I can't. Current models are incapable of producing the overabundance of matter verses antimatter in our universe.*

Defense: *So creationism, you say, is lacking because it can't explain God's creative methods, and yet your models can't verify your findings. Let's move on to the anthropic and the infinite galaxies theories. What's the usual life span of one of these galaxies that appears from nothing?*

Witness: *A few thousand years at most—it would be extremely unstable.*

Defense: *In current evolutionary thought, how long does it take to create DNA?*

Witness: *Several billion years.*

Defense: *Several billion years? That means, according to evolutionary time lines, life could never form in one of these galaxies. Wow. Professor, I think we really have uncovered some incisive clues about origins.*

In 1995, a popular movie with no on-screen actors or actresses won an Academy Award. Twenty-seven animators created one of the most amazingly real-looking graphic movies ever made up to that point. Produced on a budget of $30 million, the film earned nearly $200 million in the United States and more than $350 million worldwide. Although no living person appeared anywhere in the movie, it featured a stellar cast of voices including Tom Hanks's and Tim Allen's. *Toy Story* set a new standard in "cartoon" entertainment as its lovable characters set its audience wondering if the world of toys is more involved than we had imagined.

Toy Story is about a cowboy doll named Woody who has been the favorite plaything of his owner, Andy, since the boy was very young. One day, though, a birthday party concludes with Andy receiving an unexpected present. Woody's prized position among the toys is immediately challenged by the newcomer, a sizzling action figure named Buzz Lightyear. The spaceman lights up, sprouts wings, and shouts a variety of phrases at the push of a button, and his rallying cry, "To infinity and beyond!" becomes Woody's nightmare. Buzz, it seems, thinks he is not just a toy but the real spaceman who actually can traverse the galaxies. The primary storyline for the movie centers on Woody's efforts to bring Buzz back to reality and help him grasp where he really stands in light of infinity. Eventually, Buzz confronts the truth and discovers he's much better off accepting his purpose as a toy in Andy's room.

Buzz Lightyear's quest to go beyond infinity is not unlike the strange path many take in trying to factor God out of the origins equation. The reality of infinity lies at the heart of the debate about how we—and the universe—came into being, but despite claims to the contrary, naturalistic science cannot get us there.

It's Infinitude, Dude

I'll admit something most people don't like to admit: I'm getting old. However, I'm still young enough to be a little comforted by comparing myself to half the people I know. As a middle-aged man, there are still plenty of folks older than I am. So by one way of looking at it, being old depends on whom we choose for comparison.

Whether you're nine or ninety, though, you can be assured you are really young when compared to infinity. Webster's defines *infinity* as "an unlimited extent of time, space, or quantity." The word comes from the Latin *finites* that means "limited," and infinite is simply "that which is not finite, or limited." Billions of trillions of years are just a wink when we compare them to infinity.

It would seem obvious that "going beyond" infinity is a ludicrous idea. The absurdity of it, in fact, is part of what makes Buzz Lightyear's claim so humorous. In the debate over origins, however, there are those whose attempts to avoid God end up sounding as deluded as a child's toy that thinks it's an astronaut.

Putting Infinity in a Box

In trying to make sense of the reality that something has to be infinite or eternal while at the same time sidestepping the possibility that an eternal Creator is behind the universe, naturalists have come up with an imaginative array of theories to explain the situation. The various concepts offer differing ways to suggest that the universe itself is infinitely old, but each suggestion has its own set of problems.

Steady as She Goes

The steady state theory holds that the universe simply had no beginning, that it has always existed much as it is today. This approach was widely popular for many years but fell into disrepute during the 1900s thanks to the discovery of the laws of thermodynamics. The steady state theory directly violates the second law of thermodynamics, which predicts that eventually all of the energy available in the universe will be used up. So, if the universe really were infinitely old, it would have already run down long ago.

There was one valiant attempt to resuscitate the theory by explaining how new energy might come into being. Physicist Fred Hoyle strongly opposed the big bang concept because it implied a point at which the universe began, and that, in turn, could be used to imply that a God began it. Since Hoyle did not want any part of this, he hypothesized that hydrogen atoms keep coming into existence (somehow), and they keep the universe from running out of steam. Where these hydrogen atoms come from Hoyle could not tell us, and this is why most scientists now do not believe the steady state theory is a viable possibility.

Bound to Be Boundless

With the unbounded universe theory, scientists hold that a quantum-size cosmic entity they call a singularity appeared from nothing. The universe simply popped into existence with no outside force. However, this theory leads to another dead end. Actually, to be more accurate, it starts there.

To hearken back to the basic premise once again of all the reasoning in this book, we know from common experience that something cannot come from nothing. Every effect has a cause. There are no exceptions whatsoever to this observation, so there is no logical means by which to suggest such a thing has ever happened. The bottom line is that there is no proof for this theory and never will be.

Oscillating Universe Still Has Some Fans

One remaining theory continues to have many proponents today, but not because it is any more compelling than the first two. It remains only because the flaws are not as blatantly obvious as the steady state or unbounded universe options.

The oscillating universe theory, made popular by atheists, such as Carl Sagan and the late science fiction writer Isaac Asimov, suggests that the universe undergoes an infinite series of explosions and contractions. The theory addresses both the something-from-nothing quandary as well as the fact that an infinite universe would run down. Their answer in a nutshell is that we are one of an infinite series of past universes. This is how it works: After the big bang, everything would expand to a certain point, and then the mass of all the material in the universe would pull itself back together again. The never-ending expansion and contraction continues through an infinite number of cycles in a process that has been nicknamed the big crunch.

As I said, the problems with this theory are not as instantly apparent, but they are, nevertheless, insurmountable. Despite the intent, the theory has not completely satisfied the second law of thermodynamics. One of the law's implications is that no real physical process can finish with as much useful energy as it had to start with. Some energy is always wasted. This means the universe as a perpetual motion machine is impossible because little by little, energy will be lost. Once or twice may not matter, but if this happens an infinite number of times, somewhere along the line, all energy will be lost, and the process will stop.

Second, there are no known physics that will reverse the expansion and cause a new explosion. Even if all of the matter could be sucked back into a single glob, no one has shown a plausible cause for it to explode again.

The third problem is that the universe does not contain enough mass to reverse the expansion anyway. Galaxies and their stars, nebulae, planets, and moons are all moving away from one another too fast to ever come back together again. The momentum of the expansion is so great that the combined gravitational pull of all the material is not sufficient to stop the movement and bring things together. And there's no other force that could bring about a collapse. It has been shown that at the universe's rate of expansion, it will not collapse back in on itself. Hence, a big crunch will never happen.

Rather than toward a big crunch, the second law of thermodynamics leads us more toward a big fizzle. From a strictly naturalistic viewpoint, the future of the universe is very cold. In 10 to 13 billion years, the cosmos will consist of 90 percent dead stars, 9 percent supermassive black holes, and 1 percent atomic matter. Eventually, material in this dark, cold, still-expanding universe will be reduced to an ultrathin gas of elementary particles and radiation. Elementary-particle physics shows that protons, at this point, will decay into electrons and positrons, and space will be filled with a rarified gas so thin that the distance between an electron and a positron will be the distance between one end of our galaxy and the other—one hundred thousand light years. That's a very thin gas. There will be nothing to bring it back together again.

The logical question at this stage of our discussion would be: Who in the world could still believe the universe is in some way eternal? And the logical answer, of course, should be: no one. Even though science has only recently proven the impossibility of an eternal physical universe, the logical perception that it is not eternal has been around for a long time.

The Kalam Argument

One of the strongest arguments that the universe is not eternal is called the *kalam* cosmological argument (kalam is an Arabic word that means "eternal"). Plato (428–347 BC) was a philosopher in Athens who developed a rudimentary form of this argument. Simply stated, the kalam argument says, "Because the universe is *not* eternal, it is not infinitely old and therefore must have a cause." The kalam argument points to God as that Cause.

That everything has a cause is a reasonable assertion, and the Bible, in Psalm 90:2, explains a bit more about who this Cause is: "Before the mountains were born, before You gave birth to the earth and the world, even from eternity to eternity, You are God." Moses, the writer of this particular psalm, taught that God has no beginning. He exists from ever-lasting to everlasting, from infinity to infinity—forever.

Even Genesis 1:1, the opening verse of the Bible we talked about in chapter 5, is based on the premise that God has always existed. "In the beginning," it says, "God created the heavens and the earth." In order to get things started, God had to have been around already. If it could be proven that the universe is the thing that is infinite, then God wouldn't have to be. But as we've pointed out, contemporary science clearly says our universe is finite. It is God who exists from infinity past to infinity future.

Telescopes Point to a Beginning

In the 1920s, as I've already discussed, the work of astronomer Edwin Hubble revealed that the universe is spreading out at an amazing rate in every direction. This phenomenon was confirmed by many notable scientists of his day, including Albert Einstein. As a result, virtually every prominent scientist agrees that cosmic expansion is a reality. I've also described the big bang theory, which has grown out of the discovery of the expanding universe, so let me draw one further implication of the theory as we talk about God as the Cause of everything.

The big bang is like a rock dropping in a pond. Waves move outward from the point of impact with the water's surface. If we were to trace all the waves in our expanding universe back to where they started, we would trace it to the original rock that caused this event. Scientists have coined a term for this "rock" and now call the cause of the universe the singularity. Whatever this singularity is, it is what scientists believe caused the big bang. It's the thing that exploded. As a result, the cosmological debate about origins centers on the nature of the singularity. What was it made of? How big was it? Where did it come from? And most importantly: what was there before the singularity? So far, no one has come forth with answers to these questions—at least not naturalistic ones.

Do the Math

We also know the universe had a beginning because of mathematics. It is fascinating to note that it is mathematically impossible to go back infinitely in time. An infinitely old universe is a mathematical impossibility. Let me explain.

Thanks in large measure to the Greek philosopher and mathematician Aristotle, we know a great deal about infinity. Aristotle lived from 384 to 322 BC, and we learned from him that we cannot traverse an actual infinite. An actual infinite is a complete set to which nothing can be added. It is truly infinite, but in math there are no known sets of complete infinity.

A mathematical infinite is not an actual infinite. Many people do not understand that because we can do a lot of weird things with a mathematical infinity. The seventeenth-century mathematician John Wallace made it easier for us to play around with infinity by inventing a symbol for it—it looks like an eight turned sideways—and if we take the symbol for infinity and use it as an integer (a number), we can do peculiar computations.

Let's say we have a set of numbers such as all numbers 1 through 10. Even though we've put boundaries on the set, there is nevertheless an infinite quantity of numbers between 1 and 10. You can always find another number between any two in the set. But 1 through 10 is not the only infinite set of numbers. What if I take another set such as even whole numbers (2, 4, 6, 8, etc.)? Which group is bigger—1 through 10 or even whole numbers? The answer, of course, is neither. They both are the same size—infinitely large. And what if I take that first set of infinite numbers and divide it by two? Which is larger—the original set or the sub-divided set? Again, they are the same. It does not matter what I do to an infinite set of numbers because they are merely an infinite *potential*, never an actual infinite. Every set of infinite numbers will be the same size. A potential infinite can never become an actual infinite. With a potential infinite, we try to get an infinite by addition. However, it is impossible to count to an actual infinite because we can always add one more. Infinity is always another number away.

Some say the universe has an infinite past, but that is the same as saying, "I have counted back to infinity." It doesn't work. Any point in the past is a finite time, no matter how many billions of years we might rewind the tape. There's always more time ago.

The same is true of distance, too, by the way. If I take off in a rocket ship, planning to stop when I have flown an infinite distance, I will never stop. There's always farther to travel. So if the universe came to us from an infinite distance in time or space, it would never make it to our current position. And if it does make it to where we are now, mathematically that means only one thing—that it started from a finite distance or time past.

Clearly this means the universe started at some point of time. Which also means that time itself had a beginning. And that, in turn, means time as well as space was created—it was *caused*. That is exactly what the Bible teaches. God, who always was, created everything that is, including time, space, and matter. Big as it is, the universe is a great, long, *finite* linear chain. Everything that now is was preceded by the things that were. The world as it is now was caused by the world as it was yesterday, and that world was caused by the way it was before that and so on. Because we cannot go back infinitely, we will get to what is called a first cause.

There Is a Cause Because

Think for a moment about that first cause. We can deduce several conclusions about it, using, of course, our principle that we should assume our observations to be logically based on what we see around us:

- The first cause has to be uncaused in order to cause everything else. That is an incredible idea, but the notion of a designer God is the only rational explanation for such a thing. We've proven that nothing physical and no aspect of the universe could be that first cause.

- This cause had to exist outside the universe. The universe did not make itself so if the first cause created the universe, the cause cannot be the universe.

- The cause had to exist outside of time since the first cause created time itself. We know from Einstein that time is relative. It is related to space, gravity, and matter. Without these three entities, there is no time. Hence, the Cause is beyond all these created things.

- The first cause is magnificently powerful—powerful enough to create a universe we cannot fathom.

So why must we come to the conclusion that the first cause is the God of the Bible? The primary reason is that a first cause great enough to create the universe is more than a *mechanical* cause; it is a *volitional* cause.

A mechanical cause happens when the wind blows an object, and the object moves. The process is the simple physics of cause and effect—something pushes an object so it moves.

Volitional cause, on the other hand, is the result of a will being exerted. This requires a conscious choice. So mechanical cause is not possible before anything exists on which the mechanics can operate. A willful cause is needed to start things off. In addition, the design and apparent purpose we observe suggests a cause of the will. So logically, the God of design, the Elohim of Scripture, is the most apparent first cause.

To Actual Infinity and Beyond!

Only God is an actual infinite. God is right here in my chair, for example, and he is in my automobile, my house, your house, and wherever you happen to be reading this book. Yes, he is everywhere. Christian theology calls this omnipresence, and in Psalm 139:8 the Bible says it like this: "If I go up to heaven, You are there; if I make my bed in Sheol, You are there." There is no place I can go that God is not. He is the only actual infinite in the universe.

In real life, though, there are lots of Buzz Lightyears who think they can get their arms (and minds) around infinity. At best, though, they're merely playing with potential infinities.

Many people are confused about who they really are, confused about who their Master really is. The most startling revelation anyone could have in this life is when he or she realizes the finiteness of man versus the infinity of God—that we, the caused things, came about thanks to One who had no cause.

Unless that's the starting point, nothing else will make sense. Everything is contingent on accepting that reality. That's why our discussion of contingency is next.

CHAPTER SEVEN

Evidence from Contingency – It *All* Depends

Defense Attorney: *Metaphysics. That's the line of reasoning the prosecution has been promoting—under the guise of science. It's a philosophy based solely on what is outside the realm of objective experience. In other words, the claims of metaphysics are beyond proof. A metaphysical claim is true, so its proponents claim, merely because they say so. As we've seen, the prosecution's approach to origins is purely metaphysical, offering no verifiable or logically consistent evidence for the origin of the universe. It is this lack of evidentiary footing that leaves the case open to our contention that all things are contingent upon a beginning source. The defense, on the other hand, readily admits we are attempting to prove things none of us can see physically. However, we hold to respected principles of logic to draw our conclusions; for instance, it is rational to deduce that things that are caused are dependent— contingent—on an ultimate cause.*

Prosecution: *The remarks of the defense notwithstanding, at this time we will remind the jury that evolution has been granted judicial notice by this court as the best explanation for life's origin and progression. We enumerated the three pillars of naturalistic evolution: descent with modification, natural selection, and variation. In refuting the defense's argument for contingency, we will specifically focus on the second and third pillars of Darwinian thought.*

Variation or mutation is the key provision for increasing a given creature's capacity to survive and multiply. Natural selection, the survival of the fittest, is the catalytic force of the evolutionary clock—a force so potent that scientists cite it as the chief architect of nature's engineering and biological wonders such as the eye and the wing. In its arguments for intelligent design, the defense alleged that the hominids, ape-men, were nothing more than the stuff of pseudoscience or fraud. The prosecution flatly denies such allegations and offers five intermediary sequences of Coelacanth, Seymouria, Therapsida, Basilosaurus, and Archaeopteryx. These species represent powerful links within the evolutionary chain and demonstrate nature's independent, built-in ability to live, thrive, and adapt to any environment.

I love to work jigsaw puzzles. Piece by piece, as the puzzle comes together a coherent picture takes shape. Part of the fun is the detective work of finding the right piece at the right time, and part is the satisfaction of seeing the entire image assembled. What makes the puzzle possible in the first place, though, is that all the individual pieces fit together. That's what the puzzle box top means when it calls them interlocking pieces. No one piece or group of pieces stands alone. The place of each piece is contingent on other pieces. The jigsaw puzzle is another of those everyday observations helpful in reasoning through things we can't observe—like the necessity of God behind the pieces of creation.

A Brief History of Contingency

Over the centuries, many observers have noticed the universe is like a gigantic multidimensional puzzle in which all the pieces fit together with astonishing precision to make the cosmos function. Many scholars, scientists, and philosophers have come to see this as potent evidence for the existence of God, and the only way naturalists today can get around this reality is to ignore the issue of contingency. Things fit together with other things, and without those other things, nothing works. The whole couldn't have come about gradually because so many components depend on each other.

The argument from contingency is well established. The famed thirteenth-century philosopher and theologian Thomas Aquinas first popularized the idea. Aquinas was known as the "angelic doctor" because he developed a sophisticated theology of angels (he's the one who asked the famous question, "How many angels can fit on the head of a pin?"). He lived from 1225 to 1274 and is most renowned for his massive, sixty-volume work *Summa Theologica*. In the second volume, addressing the nature and existence of God, Aquinas advanced five proofs theologians have come to call the cosmological argument for the existence of God. The line of reasoning delivers five devastating blows to an atheistic worldview, and the third of these evidences is the argument from contingency we will explore shortly.

Another philosopher, René Descartes, who lived from 1596 to 1650, was also a physicist and mathematician. He set about to prove the argument from contingency but began by systematically doubting everything—even his own existence. What he concluded was that he must exist because he was able to think about his existence. Descartes claimed if anyone doubts his existence, it actually proves he exists because the thought process required by doubting is itself the proof of existence. He presented this argument in his discourse on method and arrived at his infamous statement: *Cogito ergo sum*—"I think, therefore I am."

More recently, F. C. Copleston, a brilliant expert on Thomas Aquinas, has furthered the argument of contingency in his books *Aquinas, Medieval Philosophy, and A History of Philosophy*. Copleston used the contingency argument most effectively against Bertrand Russell, the famous agnostic, in a public debate. Broadcast in 1948 on the BBC, it was reprinted later in Russell's 1957 book *Why I Am Not a Christian*.

Despite their significant contributions to the subject, however, Aquinas, Descartes, and Copleston did not invent the argument from contingency. The history of this argument goes all the way back to the first century AD when the apostle Paul presented contingency thinking in Acts 17:22–30.

Paul argued contingency in Athens, Greece, the intellectual capital of the ancient world. The smartest people from the known world would gather in Athens—the home of Socrates, Plato, and Aristotle—where they met routinely at the acropolis on Mars Hill. There, Paul offered the famous speech recorded in Acts 17. The account of his speech mentioned the Epicureans and Stoics as some of the philosophers present that day. The Epicureans were followers of Epicurus who died in Athens in 270 BC. He taught that life is short and ends in nothingness, so we should have a ball and try to avoid pain at all cost because pleasure is the chief goal of a human being. The Stoics were founded by Zeno and flourished about 300 BC. Zeno taught that life is pain, but God is everything and someday God will absorb us. Other philosophers heard Paul, and many of them did not believe in God but did believe in a premodern form of naturalistic evolution. The Athenians, in fact, thought themselves superior to other peoples because Athenians believed they originally came from the ground. Others believed man came from a white worm that crawled out of the river.

Paul's essential argument to the Athenian group was that man is contingent. In verse 25b, Paul said God "gives everyone life and breath and all things." And in verse 26, he proclaimed, "From one man He has made every nation of men to live all over the earth and has determined their appointed times and the boundaries of where they live." He pointed to a specific contingency (Adam) on which the rest of the human race depends. God's plan is so elaborate that he determined who each of us would be, when we would be born, our family, race, and sex—everything about us.

Paul even referenced some of his audience's favorite thinkers. In verse 28, he cited two prominent Greek poets of the time to underscore the argument that human beings are dependent and contingent: "For in Him we live and move and exist, as even some of your own poets have said, 'For we are also His offspring.'"

People Are Contingent

Contingent means "the state of being dependent upon something else for existence." People, for example, are contingent beings. You and I require others as the explanation for why we exist. You have parents. Your parents had parents, and their parents had parents. A birth certificate proves you were born, contingent on the lives and relationship of others. Every human is a contingent being, and we share several characteristics with all other contingent beings:

1. A contingent thing has not always been here. Anything that had a beginning is contingent.

2. It is possible for contingent beings to cease to exist. If they can die, they are contingent beings.

3. The world is possible without any given contingent creature. If all of us contingent creatures were to disappear right now, would the world continue? Some might say no, but it is probable that the world would go on.

4. Contingent beings can be prevented from existing by altered circumstances. Let's say my mother and father never got together. Without their relationship, I wouldn't be. So, if there is a set of circumstances that could have caused me not to come into being, I am contingent.

5. Contingent beings depend on other things for existence. Do we need oxygen, water, and food? Of course.

Every person on this planet is contingent, and that has staggering ramifications. Every contingent being has a cause outside itself. So, if the world were ever totally empty in the past, then it would be empty forever because if everything is contingent, then nothing would now exist if there was ever a time at which nothing existed. What we observe, though, is a world that is not empty, and we see that contingent beings do exist (I know that I exist—*Cogito ergo sum*). We've also already shown there was a time when the universe began. That means there was a time before the beginning when there was nothing. Something or someone has to not be contingent, or we wouldn't be here.

The Noncontingent One

In order for any of us to exist, there has to be a Being who is not contingent and who is responsible for bringing all contingent beings into existence. That is the point Paul made in Acts 17:24–25 when he claimed, "The God who made the world and everything in it—He is Lord of heaven and earth and does not live in shrines made by hands. Neither is He served by human hands, as though He needed anything, since He Himself gives everyone life and breath and all things." Contingent beings need stuff; noncontingent beings need nothing.

So absolute is the noncontingent being's needing nothing that the apostle Paul made the following remarkable points:

- God is self-sufficient. An expert in the Old Testament, Paul may well have had Psalm 50:10–12 in mind: "For every animal of the forest is Mine, the cattle on a thousand hills. I know every bird of the mountains, and the creatures of the field are Mine. If I were hungry, I would not tell you, for the world and everything in it is Mine."

- The world is not possible without God. Here is a big

difference between us and God. The world is possible without us but not without God. Aquinas put it this way: "There must be at least one necessary being"—One necessary for all contingent matter to exist. Instead of calling it a noncontingent being, Aquinas called it "necessary," but the bottom line is that there has to be a necessary, noncontingent being to account for all the contingent beings. Only the noncontingent being is required for the world to exist.

· God is the originator of the universe. Everyone else has had the gift of existence passed on from another, and if we follow the chain of being, we end up at a necessary being that created us, the contingent beings. The noncontingent Being is perhaps best described by himself in Exodus 3:14a: "I AM WHO I AM." He defines himself by himself because there is no other like him. He is the Originator of all things.

The Unmade Maker

The apostle Paul also pointed out what should be obvious but is important to make clear: Man did not make God. In a satirical twist on Christian teaching, some naturalists have said, "Man made God in his image." Paul addressed this idea in Acts 17:29, where he proclaimed God is not "fashioned by human art and imagination." Man did not make up God. F. C. Copleston, who dismantled Bertrand Russell in his debate, also weighed in on the point: "You could add up the contingent beings to infinity and it still would not equal one necessary being." [1]

Paul reasoned, in fact, that we are so dependent on God that we depend on him for life itself. You and I are dependent on him for breath. You have a set of lungs you did not craft for yourself. If you were hospitalized and hooked up to a respirator, you wouldn't accuse the medical technician who operates the machine of not existing, yet that is the approach many people take toward God. The reason we get our perception of God's origin turned around is that man is lost, not God. It's almost as if we think he is contingent on us. But the truth is, not only are each of us contingent on him, everything is.

All-Around Contingency

In addition to the contingency of people, the apostle taught that the universe is contingent. He wrote in Acts 17:24a that God is the One "who made the world and everything in it." Even apart from the Bible's claim that God caused the universe, though, a reasoned argument suggests there are only three possibilities about where the universe came from: (1) it's always been here, (2) it came from nothing, and (3) God made it.

In our discussion of cause in chapter 6, we addressed the idea "it's always been here" and how the second law of thermodynamics guarantees that the universe is not eternal. We've also explained the illogic of thinking the universe might have come about spontaneously from nothing. Our experience does not support any contention along those lines.

The key is that if something exists (i.e., the universe), there must exist, whatever it is, that which is required to make things exist. For example, a rock is made of various compounds, but these compounds must exist *before* the rock is made or else there can be no rock.

Since we know that the universe is, then there must be what it takes for the universe to exist. The cosmos is inadequate to bring itself about. Another facet of the contingency of the universe is that whatever it takes for the universe to exist cannot be identical to itself. This, of course, is simply an extension of the observation that, while one contingent thing can bring about another, the chain of contingent things must end at some point with a thing that is not contingent. Otherwise, it would be the equivalent of my saying, "I didn't have parents. I caused myself." No one would buy that statement, and yet that is the logic of those who believe the universe is self-caused or even that the current universe was caused by a previous universe that caused itself.

It is similarly true that no part of a contingent thing—including the atoms and molecules from which it is made—can be the cause of the whole. It makes no more sense to argue that hydrogen atoms created the universe than it does for me to suggest my arm made me.

The Lost Puzzle Piece

Few things are more frustrating than working for days on a jigsaw puzzle only to discover that one of the pieces is missing. It keeps me from completing the picture. What many people—especially naturalists—fail to recognize is that the crucial piece they are missing from the puzzle of the cosmos is God. So the picture never quite makes sense. The problem is nowhere more dramatically evident than in naturalistic attempts to explain contingencies through evolution. Hugely significant pieces are missing from the puzzle. Here is what some evolutionists have to say on the subject:

- *Mark Ridley*, zoologist: "No real evolutionist uses the fossil record as evidence in favor of evolution over creation." [2]

- *Stephen Jay Gould*: "The fossil record, with its abrupt transitions, offers no support for gradual change." The problem has been evident for quite some time because Gould had said twenty years earlier in the May 1977 issue of *Natural History*: "The evolutionary trees that adorned our textbooks have data only at the tips and nodes of their branches. The rest is inference, however reasonable, but not the evidence of fossils." [3]

- *David B. Kitts*: "Evolution requires intermediate forms between species, and paleontology does not provide them." [4]

Steven Stanley: "The known fossil record fails to document a single example of phyletic evolution." [5]

- *E. J. H. Corner*, botany professor and evolutionist: "To the unprejudiced, the fossil record of plants is in favor of special creation." [6]

- *J. R. Norman*: "The geological record has so far provided no evidence as to the origin of the fishes." [7]

- *A. S. Romer*: "The origin of rodents is obscure. No transitional forms are known." [8]

- *Roger Lewin*: "The [evolutionary] transition to the first mammal...is still an enigma." [9]

- *Lyall Watson*: "The fossils that decorate our family tree are so scarce that there are still more scientists than specimens...The remarkable fact is that all the physical evidence that we have for human evolution can still be placed—with room to spare—inside a single coffin." [10]

The truth is the pieces of the naturalist's evolutionary puzzle will never be found because only the God piece of the puzzle can make our understanding of the universe and its origins fit together.

A Fitting Solution

Acts 17:25 tells us God gives life and breath to all things. Evidence abounds that this is true. Complex organs are far too sophisticated to have arisen through blind, random change. In chapter 5, we discussed the overwhelming complexity of the human eye. But think for a moment what the mere existence of the eye presupposes. It assumes that light exists. Since the eye is an organ developed specifically to cope with and process light, it is as if the eye's originating force already knew light is a factor of existence that a living being needs to have the capacity to handle. The eye makes the assumption of light. Although scientists even now cannot fully explain what light is, evolution teaches that the eye (somehow developed by chance) understood how to process, use, and convert light into intelligent information.

Ears, too, are similarly sophisticated. They process invisible sound waves, converting energy into intelligible information the brain can comprehend. Ears assume sound.

Lungs, another sophisticated organ, assume air. And with lungs, there is no option of trial and error. Evolution would have to get lungs right on the first try. Otherwise, the breathing of any animal in which the part was installed would fail, and the creature would die. Since lungs are perfectly suited to process air, lungs point to a Creator who would get it right the first time.

The interaction between various species of plants and animals also represents contingency at work. In his book *The Unselfish Green Gene*, Dr. David Demick explained that plants sustain the human animal world. He pointed out, though, that the plant world is biochemically superior to the human and animal worlds because plants can get by on so much less than we can. All they need is sunlight, carbon dioxide, and water. Plants balance the biosphere in a way that makes us contingent on them.[11] With all their nutritional and medicinal uses, it is as though the plant world was made for man.

The intricacy of the way so many contingencies fit together is mind-boggling. In one sense, it could even be considered miaculous. Miracles, though, deserve special treatment since they constitute yet another compelling evidence for God. That's why we'll focus on them specifically in chapter 8.

CHAPTER EIGHT

Miracles, for Real

Prosecutor: *Your Honor, the prosecution respectfully submits that continuation of this trial is a waste of the court's time. These proceedings pit religious beliefs against scientific laws. It's apples to oranges—two entirely separate realms of thought.*

Defense Attorney: *What's the matter, counsel? Is a competing and competent line of reasoning getting to be too much for you to handle?*

Prosecutor: *Hardly. Your Honor, natural laws such as gravity and motion govern the universe. To embrace miracles or creationism, however, natural laws must be thrown out. After all, laws of nature don't allow for people coming back to life, amputees sprouting new limbs, or invisible cosmic beings speaking a universe into existence.*

Defense: *Excuse me. There's no reason we shouldn't be allowed to go the distance with our lines of argument. The defense can show clearly that we are not dealing with irreconcilable thought processes.*

Prosecutor: *Then you've got your work cut out for you. The National Academy of Sciences argued this point in its amicus brief filed with the Fifth Circuit Court of Appeals by seventy-two Nobel laureates, seventeen state academies of science, and seven other scientific organizations in Edwards v. Aguillard. The defense's approach here is nothing more than glossed over "creation science," which according to the academy cannot meet the criteria of true science because "science relies entirely upon naturalistic explanations." It has no concern with "supernatural or occult explanations."* [1] *The prosecution maintains, as Scottish historian and philosopher David Hume has noted, "A miracle is a violation of the laws of nature," laws that are a "firm and unalterable experience."* [2] *At this time, the prosecution requests summary judgment.*

Defense: *Your Honor, this is a priori. The academy has redefined science so no one can argue with them. Science is based on empirical research and impartial conclusions— whether its results point to natural or supernatural causes.*

On one of our family vacations, we made a souvenir stop at a great "magic" store. Being a fan of magic tricks, I bought all kinds of cool stuff. I love performing some of the tricks I found, and now I can actually impress a few people with my little show. But people are impressed only as long as they don't know the secret of how the ruse works. If they figure out the mystery, a trick is not nearly so magic anymore.

Whether or not people know the secret of a magic trick, though, virtually no one would mistake a magician for a miracle worker. Magic tricks aren't miracles. Everyone knows they are simply some sort of manipulation of the usual way things happen. There is a monumental difference between magic and miracles. Harry Houdini is known as the greatest magician who ever lived, but he was never thought to have performed a miracle.

Miracles Make the Case

To present the distinction simplistically, it is possible to find out how a magic trick is performed, but no one can figure out a miracle. That is actually one of the main points of a miracle. It is supposed to register with us as something for which the only explanation is that God intervened in an unusual way. God does miracles as a catalyst for faith. They are supposed to point people to him, and if a person is open to the possibility, that's exactly what they do.

Here's the rub, though, in talking about miracles. Some people simply choose for no substantial reason to believe miracles aren't possible. Again, applying the same standard of reasoning used throughout this book, we can show that interpreting certain events as supernaturally caused miracles is a completely rational conclusion.

A skeptic confronted me once, saying, "I don't believe God can do miracles." I responded, "If there is a God, he would be able to do miracles." What the skeptic really was trying to say is, "I don't believe in miracles because I don't believe there is a God." When I pointed out the fallacy in his statement, he admitted, "Yeah, that's right." The way he had originally announced his position put the cart before the horse. Belief or nonbelief in God always comes *before* belief or nonbelief in miracles. The two reasons for this are very straightforward:

1. If there is no God, there is no one who can do miracles, so miracles do not occur.

2. If there is a God, he is capable of working miracles, so miracles can possibly—and probably do—occur.

The skeptic's position makes no sense. God, by anyone's definition, is capable of doing miracles, so it is an absurdity to suggest he *can't* do miracles even if he does exist. If he can't do miracles, then he's not God, and God, as such, does not exist.

The burden of proof in using miracles as evidence for God does not rest on whether he is capable of the miraculous. It rests on whether miracles happen. If it can be shown beyond any reasonable doubt that miracles have occurred, then the only explanation is that a God also exists who caused the miracles. On the other hand, the only way to prove that miracles do not and cannot occur is to prove that God does not exist. And as should be quite clear by this point in our case, that proposition is seriously in doubt.

So remember, there's no getting around it: if evidence indicate that miracles have occurred, God must exist. That's the formula.

Miracles under Attack

Although for much of history, miracles have been widely accepted as a genuine part of human experience, in the seventeenth century, the intellectual movement known as the Enlightenment made it popular to question the validity of miracles. Previously in Western civilization, the Bible was considered the universal authority in all fields of knowledge, but the penchant of many Enlightenment scholars for rationalism—which was not always rational—brought the Bible under attack by atheists, deists, and even some liberal churchmen.

David Hume, a Scottish philosopher and leader during the Enlightenment, proclaimed miracles to be in violation of natural laws, and therefore "as a firm and unalterable experience established these laws, the proof is against a miracle." [3]

Another Enlightenment thinker, Voltaire announced, "A miracle is the violation of mathematical, divine, immutable, eternal laws and, therefore, is a contradiction." [4] But why were these skeptics so anxious to attack miracles?

As I said, the reasons are not necessarily logical, because they sidestep the issue of whether or not a God exists who could break natural laws to cause a miracle. They screen out the possibility of the supernatural, which assures that they will *not* find any way to have miracles occur within their purely naturalistic worldview.

Skeptics instinctively recoil at miracles and must find a way to negate them. A miracle is a special act of God that interrupts the natural course of events. Antony Flew said, "A miracle is something which would have never happened had nature, as it were, been left to its own devices." [5] If miracles happen, it is checkmate—end of story.

The Testimony of Miracles

People sometimes throw the word *miracle* around in ways that do not help create a clear understanding of what a miracle actually is. Some things are amazing, but they are not miracles. A miracle is not a skin cream that makes wrinkles vanish. It's not scoring three touchdowns in a fourth-quarter comeback to win the Super Bowl. And it's not even a jumbo jet about which we marvel, "I don't know how that thing flies!" There are explanations of how each of these things happens. A miracle is an unexplainable act of God, and the best resource anywhere for finding a wealth of information about miracles is the Bible.

In Acts 2:22, the apostle Peter preached a powerful sermon in which he proposed: "Men of Israel, listen to these words: This Jesus the Nazarene was a man pointed out to you by God with miracles, wonders, and signs that God did among you through Him, just as you yourselves know." God confirmed his truth through a trinity of miracles Peter called "miracles, wonders, and signs."

Hebrews 2:4 also explains that signs, wonders, and miracles were used to confirm the gospel. The Greek word *semeion* means specifically "a *miraculous* sign." The word connotes that the thing is a signal. Its use in the Bible implies that God has placed signals—billboards—all through history. The signs tell us he is there and ultimately point the way to salvation. As such, miracles are part of the salvation history of mankind.

Many people, when they read the biblical accounts of miracles, wish they had lived during the Bible times because they believe there were more miracles then. But even in the Bible miracles are actually quite rare. They cluster around four major periods in biblical history.

First, we find them about 1500 BC during the time of the Exodus and Moses. The plagues on Egypt and the parting of the Red Sea were among the most famous miracles that occurred during this period. A second grouping of miracles occurred during the time of the kings in the ninth century BC. Two major miracle-working prophets, Elijah and Elisha, wowed kings and ordinary folks alike with God's wonders.

The third spate of miracles centered on Jesus Christ. Check with any encyclopedia, any multivolume collection of information, or any survey on the subject of miracles, and we will find that it is almost universally accepted that Jesus was the greatest miracle worker in history. There's not even a close second. Jesus Christ was so recognized as a miracle worker that King Herod wanted to meet him merely to see what amazing feats he might do (Luke 23:8). Not even Jesus's bitterest enemies denied his miracles. The best they could do was to try to put a stop to his work by killing him. That even his opponents didn't deny his workings of miracles is strong evidence that the miracles really occurred. And if they did occur, what does that mean? Remember the formula. It means God exists.

It would be a dizzying task indeed to try and refute Jesus's many miracles. The New Testament documents thirty-six different ones performed by Jesus Christ. Here's a complete list:

1. The feeding of the five thousand (the only miracle recorded in all four gospels)
2. Walking on water
3. Healing of the disciple Peter's mother-in-law
4. Healing of the man with leprosy
5. Healing of the paralyzed man
6. Healing of the man with a shriveled hand
7. Calming of the storm
8. Exorcism of the Gadarene demoniac

9. The raising of Jairus's daughter

10. Healing the hemorrhaging woman

11. Exorcism of a demon-possessed boy

12. Healing of two blind men

13. Exorcism from a distance of the Canaanite woman's daughter

14. The feeding of the four thousand

15. The fig tree withering

16. Exorcism of a possessed man in the synagogue

17. Healing at a distance of the Roman centurion's servant

18. Exorcism of a blind mute and a possessed man

19. Healing of a deaf mute

20. Healing of a blind man at Bethesda

21. Healing of two blind men

22. Exorcism of a mute and a possessed man

23. The coin found in the fish's mouth

24. The first catch of fish

25. Reviving the widow's son

26. Exorcism of Mary Magdalene

27. Healing of a crippled woman

28. Healing of a man with dropsy

29. Healing at a distance of ten men with leprosy

30. Healing of a high priest's servant

31. Turning water into wine

32. Healing at a distance of an official's son at Capernaum

33. Healing of a sick man at the pool of Bethesda

34. Healing of a blind man

35. Bringing Lazarus back from the dead

36. The second catch of fish

In sum, the four gospels record seventeen healing events,

seven exorcisms, three miracles of precognition (nature), three bringing-back-from-the-dead miracles, and six nature miracles. The nature miracles are especially amazing because there we find:

- the creation of matter in the multiplication of food,
- the defiance of gravity in walking on water,
- the control of thermal energy in the calming of a storm,
- the control of the metabolic process in the withering of the fig tree, and
- the rearrangement of molecular structure and creation of matter by turning water into wine.

Finally, the fourth period of miracles centered on the founding of the early church. God used signs, wonders, and miracles to confirm the work of the apostles.

The Bible's Solid Evidence for Miracles

If skeptics write off biblical accounts of miraculous happenings as nonsense or myth, it's not because it is reasonable to do so. By any standard of evidence, the Bible substantiates beyond a reasonable doubt the miracles it records. While some may try to undermine the validity of the Bible itself, that approach is born out of ignorance of the facts. The Bible is the most well-established historical document of any kind (but a detailed discussion of the Bible's reliability is beyond the scope of our discussion here). So here are the reasons the Bible's accounts of miracles should be taken at face value and accepted as fact:

- The miracles were done in public where everyone could see them.
- Most were performed in the presence of unbelievers and skeptics—the people most likely to doubt them—not only in the presence of those biased in favor of Christ's ministry.

- They were done over a span of time, not as if a miracle worker simply "got lucky" now and then. Whether it was at the time of Moses, Elijah, Elisha, Jesus, or the early church, these miracles were done over a long enough period of time to open the miracles to serious investigation. Someone could have scrutinized events to see if the perpetrators were doing magic instead of miracles, but that never happened.
- The miracles of healing include testimonies of those who were cured. People were healed of congenital blindness, lameness, leprosy, and other afflictions, and all offer their testimonies.
- Those healed testified to being cured instantly and completely.
- When Jesus said, "Which is easier: to say, 'Your sins are forgiven you,' or to say, 'Get up and walk'? But so you may know that the Son of Man has authority on earth to forgive sins"— He told the paralyzed man, 'I tell you: get up, pick up your stretcher, and go home'" (Luke 5:23–24).
- Miracles were predicted in the Bible.
- They were beyond explanation. The healing of congenital blindness, lame people, leprosy, feeding of the five thousand, calming a storm, walking on water, and the Resurrection defy explanation.
- These miracles were so powerful that they convinced many people to follow Christ. Later, witnesses to miracles joined the church because signs confirmed the apostles' message.
- The accounts are authentic. If we read miracle narratives from other sources, we often see they are only legends. Historical figures tried to make themselves sound better than they were. Alexander the Great, for instance, hired a biographer to tell everyone how great he was and to exaggerate and stretch the truth. Augustus did the same thing. But the Bible reveals the biblical characters' warts and their bad sides. No one looks like a superhero. The

accounts are too real for that—an evidence that they tell the truth.

- Reliable records preserve the accounts of miracles. The Bible we have today is the Bible as originally written. As I mentioned earlier, it is the most well preserved of all historic documents. We know the Old Testament is reliable, for example, in part because the Dead Sea Scrolls, discovered in 1947 and dating from the third century BC to the first century AD, show the Old Testament to be accurately preserved when compared to modern versions. The New Testament evidence is equally confirming. Twenty-seven thousand copies and fragments of the Greek New Testament have been found, and when they're assembled they substantiate our modern Bible.

There's No Denying Miracles

Miracle workers in the Bible didn't hedge their bets. When they set out to do something amazing, they did it for all to see. They called their shots. That helps explain why no first-century eyewitness ever denied that Jesus could do miracles. This is a startling and compelling fact. No one ever tried to expose Jesus as a clever magician—a Harry Houdini, a David Copperfield, or a Lance Burton—to reveal how he did his tricks.

Whenever skeptics discussed Jesus, they did not debate the reality of his miracles. They knew he performed them. They debated only about how they could stop him from doing any more!

John 11:47–48, for example, records a meeting of the religious leaders ticked off at Jesus. They worried: "What are we going to do since this man does many signs? If we let Him continue in this way, everybody will believe in Him!" Elsewhere, in John 3:2, another religious leader named Nicodemus admitted to Jesus, "No one could perform these signs You do unless God were with him." How, then, did Jesus's enemies explain that Jesus was not the Messiah? The best they could come up with was to say Jesus did miracles "by the ruler of the demons!" (Mark 3:22).

Another measure of the veracity of Jesus's miracles is the *Talmud*, a Jewish document that dates from AD 75 to AD 500. The *Talmud* is a collection of writings by Jewish scholars notably biased against Jesus. Nevertheless, the writings reference Jesus and admit he had miracle-working power. Similar to those who credited his work to the devil, the Talmud writers minimized Jesus as a sorcerer. But even this is a striking admission. They didn't deny Jesus's miracle-working power. They merely maligned the source.

Clearly, modern skeptics have no reasonable basis for denying the miracles of Jesus. If so, they find themselves in direct contradiction to first-century eyewitnesses—and guess whose testimony would carry more weight in a court of law? Lest we think the records—whether by Jesus's friends *or* enemies—are biased toward miracles because they're written by "religious" people, let me throw a secularist in the mix.

Flavius Josephus, who lived from AD 37 to 97, was a historian commissioned by the Roman emperor to write an account of that generation. A brilliant scholar, Josephus completed his work in AD 92, a book called *Jewish Antiquities*. In this book, he recounted a history of the first century and included the development of Christianity. Josephus spoke of James, the brother of Jesus, and John the Baptist (including a fascinating account of his death, describing in more depth than the Bible the political reasons for John's execution). Josephus, not a Christian, wrote for a Roman audience hostile to Christianity and yet said this of Jesus

Now there was about this time Jesus, a wise man—if it be lawfu to call him a man—for he was a doer of many wonderful works. A teacher of such men as received the truth with pleasure. He drew over to him both many of the Jews and many of the Gentiles. He was The Christ; and when Pilate, at the suggestion of the principle men among us, had condemned him to the cross, those that loved him at the first did not forsake him. For he appeared to them alive again the third day as the divine prophets had foretold. These and 10,000 wonderful things concerning him and the tribe of Christians so named for him are not extinct to this day.[6]

This first-century historian testified that (1) Jesus Christ did perform miracles, and (2) he came back to life after dying.

We Never Said It Was Natural

The word miracle in the Greek is *dynamos*, the source of the word dynamite. The Greek means "power, ability, miracle, and ruler"—literally, "an extended meaning of a person or supernatural being that has administrative power." The key word is *supernatural*. That means above natural or above nature. The word itself implies there is something beyond nature.

Because he is above and outside nature, God has two ways of revealing himself to us, and having a special means to tell us about himself shouldn't surprise us. If he's beyond nature, it would require an *unnatural* way for him to enter our experience.

The first way God showed himself is through the special revelation of salvation history. God revealed his plan to redeem mankind from sin by demonstrating the need and solution little by little through the course of history. He used a special relationship with the people of Israel to set the stage for his ultimate communication through the coming of Jesus Christ. People who help unravel the mystery of this form of revelation are called theologians.

God has another area of revelation called nature. Through

creation, God shows who he is by the remarkable complexity and design of the cosmos. This portion of God's revelation, of course, is what has consumed most of our thinking in this book. People who interpret this aspect of God's revelation are called scientists.

The two aspects of revelation work together handsomely for those open to seeing them in tandem. While some scientists give credence to theologians and are comfortable with both aspects of revelation, some seem to need to think of themselves as better than, or more intellectually savvy than, theologians. As a result, they ignore the possibility (a very unscientific approach) that both fields of inquiry can be helpful and enlightening. Often, their perspective keeps them from understanding certain obvious implications of their own area of study—as we've seen many times in the course of our discussion. Let's return for a minute to our examination of various philosophical approaches to explain why this dichotomy between science and theology is unnecessary.

Hold the Miracles If You'll Let Us

Benedict Spinoza, who lived from 1632 to 1677, was a pantheist. He believed the entire universe is God and that an impersonal God is infused through all of nature. To him, nature had a fixed and immutable order, and therefore, he would say miracles are violations of the character of nature and are impossible.

Most skeptics today do not hold to this argument because it is too easy to shoot down, but during Spinoza's time, it was very popular. Since Spinoza defined a miracle as a violation of nature, he set up his argument to be destroyed. If God created nature, then he certainly can modify it. Like building a machine, certainly the manufacturer can modify it to suit changing needs. If God wants to hit the turbo on creation, he just hits it! Since God created nature, he can adjust it—no lack of logic here.

A different challenge to miracles came from David Hume, mentioned earlier in this chapter. Remember, he said miracles are impossible simply because they defy what he considered the immutable laws of nature. Hume also dismissed the testimony of those who were witnesses to a miracle. Accordingly, Hume said, "No testimony is sufficient to establish a miracle, unless the testimony be of such a kind, that its falsehood would be more miraculous, than the fact, which it endeavors to establish."[7] Hume's reasoning was that a miracle is impossible because it is impossible.

There's something wrong with such thinking. It is called circular reasoning. A possibility is ruled out because that particular possibility is one the person wants to rule out. It's based on a preferred worldview, not on logic or scientific observation.

Hume was taken to task on the point by another great mind of his generation, William Paley. In 1794, Paley wrote *A View of the Evidences of Christianity*. In his book, Paley presented historical evidence for Christianity from miracles. He also thoroughly refuted Hume, showing how he used circular reasoning.

Hume reasoned that if something amazing occurs that does not violate the laws of nature it cannot be considered a miracle. Because the event was within the bounds of the laws of nature, an explanation of a supernatural being is not needed. He also contended that if an amazing occurrence was said to have violated the laws of nature then the occurrence would certainly be ruled as false and impossible because the laws of nature cannot be violated.

According to Hume, whether something violates nature or does not violate nature, it is still not a miracle. He presupposed a closed system that assures there can be no possibility of ever discovering anything that is truly a miracle. He set up the argument so there is no way one can win if one thinks miracles are possible—not because they are truly impossible, only because Hume said they are.

Antony Flew built on Hume's argument. He claimed the evidence leans toward there being no miracles. Flew argued that no one can prove miracles happen because they are nonrepeating events. Nature, on the other hand, offers greater evidence because it is general and repeatable.

Flew is correct, of course, in saying that miracles generally are not repeatable. This is not a cogent argument for undermining the validity of miracles, however. Many events in history have happened only once, yet given the appropriate eyewitness testimony and corroboration of records, no one doubts the events occurred—nobody questions that Julius Caesar was assassinated by the Roman senate. Actually, what makes miracles special is that they are rare, not simply that they're not repeatable.

The nonrepeatable argument, of course, can and should be used against certain aspects of naturalism. Spontaneous generation, for instance, the bedrock of evolution, says that nonlife developed into life. Not only has no one ever witnessed such a thing, it was proven scientifically to be an impossibility more than 150 years ago. In an ironic twist of logic, it would mean that the original spontaneous generation from primordial broth could have come about only by a miracle . . . which Hume would say is impossible...which means the start of evolution from nonliving matter is impossible . . . which means something out of the ordinary—supernatural—would have had to start things. So even if the primordial soup is where we began (I'm not suggesting that it is—I'm being hypothetical to make a point), it would still have taken a supernatural act to make it happen. God would have to factor into the equation.

Not surprisingly, the first miracle in the Bible is the creation. And if God created everything, then all that follows is a piece of cake.

The Greatest Escape

The man still considered to be the greatest magician of all time was born in Budapest, Hungary, in 1874. His name was Ehrich Weiss. As a child, he became known as Ehrich the Great by doing magic tricks and sideshows. Even though he was just five feet nine and had a high-pitched voice, Weiss became world famous for his death-defying escapes from underwater sealed chests, torture chambers, and straitjackets. He adopted the stage name Harry Houdini from Jean Eugene Robert-Houdin, a great French magician of the nineteenth century, and eventually took Harry Houdini as his legal name.

Although Houdini was the world's greatest illusionist, midway through his life and at the height of his fame, something happened that turned his life upside down. His mother died. This led Houdini to wonder about the ultimate question: Is there life after death? He turned to spiritualists, those who practice contacting the dead on behalf of the living, and became outraged at how he found spiritualists victimizing bereaved people. So Houdini spent thirteen years exposing their fakery. He became America's premiere ghost buster. No one was more aggressive in the quest to show spiritualism as a sham. He would visit séances and expose mediums as frauds, uncovering every famous spiritualist of his generation. In 1926, he was even called to testify before a congressional committee about investigating spiritualists.

That same year, he died on Halloween (strangely enough) at the age of fifty-two. Before Houdini passed away, he gave his wife, Bess, a secret code he planned to relay to her from beyond the grave if the dead could contact the living. He figured if anyone could do it, he would be able to. For years after that on Halloween, Bess held séances, hoping to hear from Harry. She finally stopped in 1938 because she had never heard from her dead husband.

Nevertheless, where magic ends, miracles can begin. The greatest escape artist and magician could not escape the greatest trap of all—death, but the resurrection of Jesus Christ is the greatest attested miracle of all history. Through it, Jesus demonstrated his power over death, hell, and the grave. Man's magic fails sooner or later, but God's miracles prevail for all eternity.

CHAPTER NINE

The Wake-up Call of Consciousness

Judge: *The defense's contention that the "forces of nature do not know themselves" may be presumptuous—vague at least. It could be interpreted that inanimate natural forces like wind are not self-aware or that animals are not conscious beings. On the other hand, the prosecution'assertion that animals can develop consciousness via evolution is argumentative. Therefore, the burden of proof is equal on both sides. The jury will have to decide whether the arguments are valid. Now, let's move on.*

Prosecution: *At this point, we broach the question: "What does it mean to be conscious?" The Stanford Encyclopedia of Philosophy lists eight consciousness phenomena common among many animals and humans:*

1. *pain responses, such as yelps or high-pitched squeals,*
2. *visual illusions (e.g., dreams),*
3. *neurological similarities (brain structure, functionality, and response to stimuli),*
4. *visual consciousness (responsiveness to the environment),*
5. *communicative and problem-solving behavior (relational and navigational abilities),*
6. *frustration of conscious and unconscious desires (rebellious behavior or grief),*
7. *behavioral strategies in food competition situations (how to acquire food), and*
8. *self-consciousness and theory of mind.*[1]

   Undoubtedly, the most powerful evidence for disproving the argument for God from consciousness centers on animal self-consciousness research. In citing the historic work of G. G. Gallup Jr., in which chimpanzees actually recognize themselves in a mirror—versus thinking it is another chimpanzee—the encyclopedia states: "According to Gallup, et al., (2002) 'Mirror self-recognition is an indicator of self-awareness.'" It should also be noted that mirror self-recognition research among orangutans and bottlenose dolphins has yielded similar results.

Regarding the arguments from similarity, the encyclopedia concludes: "Similarity arguments for animal consciousness...may also be bolstered...as...evolutionary continuity (homology) between species." The research proves that Darwin was right: Man is not "a little lower than the angels," but only a little higher than the apes.

Have you thought about your brain today? Probably not. The brain, after all, is something we use heavily every millisecond of our lives but generally take completely for granted. In a study of the remarkable design of the cosmos, though, the brain deserves not only a second thought, it deserves focused attention. The complexity of the human brain—and the consciousness of life it allows—ranks as one of the most *mind*-boggling elements of creation.

A Very Soft Hard Drive

To believe the brain could have evolved from chance is simply... unbelievable. Even though a brain weighs only about three pounds—roughly 2 percent of human body weight—it is an astounding piece of work. It consists of an estimated 100 billion neurons—so many that it would take more than three thousand years to count each and every one of them. These assembled neurons have one quadrillion synapses (1,000,000,000,000,000!), which means there are more connections in a human brain than there are stars in the known universe. These connections allow messages to pass from neuron to neuron, and the total length of these neural connections is about sixty-eight thousand miles. That is more than all the wiring of all of the computers in the world. Information moves around the brain at speeds of up to 268 miles per hour. Even though this soft, gooey thing is an organ in the body, its description sounds more like a turbo-charged supercomputer.

Many journals and magazines, including *National Geographic*, *Scientific American*, and *Time*, acknowledge that the most complex structure in the known universe is the brain, but that addresses only the astonishing physical attributes and capabilities of a human's gray matter. Even more baffling—and beyond the staggering data processing, informational power of the brain—is the question: how did the brain attain consciousness? Strictly speaking, there's no reason any mass of organic matter—even if it managed to become living tissue—should become aware of itself. This doesn't mean consciousness isn't necessary—it's actually essential to survival—it means there's no biological cause for consciousness to exist. Much as naturalists would like to say otherwise, science cannot answer that question of consciousness satisfactorily. They know something's there but can't quite say what it is.

The Principle of the Pea

In 1997, Jaron Lanier wrote an article in the Journal of Consciousness Studies called "Death: The Skeletal Key of Consciousness Studies" in which he noted: "There is a popular story about a princess who complains that she cannot sleep comfortably because of a single pea buried underneath layers of mattresses. That pea is consciousness in the sciences." [2]

Consciousness is the "pea" of science because it lies buried beneath the layers of physical reality, seemingly untouchable by naturalistic methods and philosophy, yet continuously making its subtle presence known. That pea gives the lie to the limitations of naturalism in explaining the world in which we live (to say nothing of the world within us), as some scientists forthrightly admit. Nick Herbert holds a PhD in physics from Stanford University and writes of this conundrum in his book *Quantum Reality*: "Science's biggest mystery is the nature of consciousness. It is not that we possess bad or imperfect theories of awareness; we simply have no such theories at all. All we know about consciousness is that it has something to do with the head rather than the foot" (emphasis added).[3]

David Chalmers, a Rhodes scholar from Oxford with a PhD in philosophy and cognitive science, is similarly open about the issue in his significant work *The Conscious Mind*: "Consciousness poses the most baffling problem in the science of the mind. There is nothing that we know more intimately than conscious experience, but there is nothing that is harder to explain. All sorts of mental phenomena have yielded to scientific investigation in recent years, but consciousness has stubbornly resisted. Many have tried to explain it, but the explanations always seem to fall short of the target."[4]

At the beginning of this chapter, I asked if you'd thought about your brain today. Since you most likely hadn't, it was a rhetorical question. Until reaching this chapter, you'd probably thought equally little about consciousness as well. And unless you ponder it for a moment, the reasons for its pealike resistance to explanation may not be obvious. To help understand why it is such a tough nut for naturalistic science to crack, the best starting point is actually a very unnaturalistic source that offers some very clear explanations as to where the marvel of consciousness comes from

The Soul Reason

In Matthew 10:28, Jesus told his followers, "Don't fear those who kill the body but are not able to kill the soul; rather, fear Him who is able to destroy both soul and body in hell."

Scripture distinguishes between the body and the soul. In the Matthew verse just quoted, Jesus suggested there is a difference between the body and the soul. People are made of at least two components—a physical body and an inner consciousness Jesus called the soul. This unseen element of our being accounts for the sense that there's more to us than meets the eye.

This biblical teaching of body and soul goes all the way back to the divine breath of Genesis 2:7: "Then the LORD God formed the man out of the dust from the ground and breathed the breath of life into his nostrils, and the man became a living being." The soul is that "seed of personhood and individual identity," that spiritual part of a human being that is believed to survive death. Mark 12:30 says, "Love the Lord your God with all your heart, with all your soul, with all your mind, and with all your strength." Matthew 10:28 indicates that the soul is not destroyed by physical death. This is why mankind is unique. From the Genesis Scripture, theologians deduce that there are not only two but three dimensions to the makeup of a human being—mind, body, and spirit. A person is a spirit, dwelling in a body and possessing a consciousness. This is much different than a one-dimensional being, like a plant. A plant has a body, but it does not have a consciousness. With this understanding as a base of operations, we can move on to consider some of the fitful naturalistic attempts to explain this part of our reality.

Every Explanation but the Right One

I've heard it waggishly said that consciousness is the annoying time between naps. In a more serious attempt at a definition, however, Merriam-Webster explains consciousness as the state of being that is characterized by one or all of four things: by sensation—alertness; by emotion—whether it is love, affection, fear, compassion, anger, or hate; by volition—that is, the power to decide, the power to choose; and by fault—to know, to reason, to remember, to use signals, to use language.

This definition brings up what philosophers and scientists recognize as the mind/body problem. There are two camps here. We've already talked about one—the theistic (biblical) approach that believes there is something beyond the body called the soul. People who believe a part of us is distinct and different from the body are called dualists. As you may guess, I am a dualist.

Another group says the body is all there is; there is nothing more. We are just a lot of chemical reactions, a result of physical processes in the material world. In case you don't recognize this stance, it is the naturalist position. Someone who believes the material is all there is and accounts for everything is called a monist.

One such monist was Francis Crick. He won a Nobel Prize for his groundbreaking work on the nature and structure of DNA. Apart from his brilliant research on DNA, though, he strayed into a speculative, metaphysical realm in a book called *The Astonishing Hypothesis: The Scientific Search for the Soul.* Anything but scientific, his book actually is a treatise on how to disprove the existence of the soul. By Crick's own admission, he wrote it to oppose religion. Throughout the book, Crick opposed the idea of the homunculus. The homunculus is the hidden persona, intelligence that superintends the brain. We could call it consciousness; we could call it the soul. However, homunculus is the scientific-sounding term Crick used even though he used it simply to say that no one has it. Instead, Crick came up with this explanation for the seat of our emotions and deepest sense of self: "You, your joys and your sorrows, your memories and your ambitions, your sense of personal identity and free will are, in fact, no more than the behavior of a vast assembly of nerve cells and their associated molecules." [5] Crick compared belief in the soul to belief in a flat earth, and he effervesced about how science will ultimately prove the soul does not exist.

The difficulty with Crick's assessment is that we have lots of evidence the world is not flat, but we have little evidence we do not have a soul. In fact, the reason this controversy arises at all is that there is so much evidence for something (the pea) that scientists feel compelled to develop an explanation for, whatever it is. Crick admitted in his work that there is no material explanation so far to explain consciousness in a human being but that he would have to hold to belief in a materialistic solution because it would be the only viable answer. Since there could not possibly be a God, he suggested, there could not be a soul.[6]

Another naturalistic approach to consciousness suggests that it is merely an illusion. Some propose that what we perceive as consciousness is merely behaviorism—our response to our environment—and that we really do not have free will. Obviously, monism is not the most attractive way to think of ourselves, but then, it's not necessarily the most rational either.

The Soul of the Matter

We, who naturalists would like to write off as unthinking religious nuts, are by no means the only people who think monism comes up short in its explanation of humanness. Many great minds have accepted the notion of dualism.

As long ago as the fifth century BC, the renowned Greek philosopher and student of Socrates, Plato taught that the mind and the body were separate. Centuries later, René Descartes also argued for the existence of the soul. Descartes battled many skeptics during the Enlightenment and is known as the father of modern philosophy. He founded the rational method of philosophical research that led him to the famous perception of existence we discussed in chapter 7, "I think, therefore, I am." Descartes claimed the existence of consciousness proves the existence of God and the existence of the soul.

More recently, Roger Penrose, an Oxford professor of mathematics, has done fascinating work in this field. With well-known Cambridge professor Stephen Hawking, Penrose co-authored *The Nature of Space and Time*, and in his own book *The Emperor's New Mind* Penrose explained that the mind is more than just a physical thing. He pointed out that it is not a computer and that processes even more complex than quantum mechanics are essential for the operation of the mind.[7]

Wilder Penfield is another classic researcher in the field of consciousness. He lived from 1891 to 1976, was an Oxford Rhodes scholar, a world-famous neurosurgeon, and founder of the Montreal Neurological Institute. Author of *Mystery of the Mind*, which tackles the subject of consciousness, he was the first doctor to undertake a systematic mapping of the brain. He discovered and used direct electrical stimulation as a technique for finding damaged areas of the brain during surgery. Most doctors today know Dr. Penfield because of his groundbreaking work in epilepsy. What is very telling about Penfield is that he began his research as a strict materialist, but after extensive study, he switched to the belief that there must be a soul. He said, "Something else finds its dwelling place between the sensory complex and the motor mechanism. There is a switchboard operator as well as a switchboard."[8]

Other doctors have come to this same conclusion. Dr. William Mayo, famous surgeon and cofounder of the Mayo Medical Clinic, observed: "The keen blade of my scalpel may never uncover the soul as a tangible part of the mystery called man, but I know that it is there. I am as confident of its presence as I am the most elemental truth to which my own medical sciences adhere."[9]

Apart from dualism, it is difficult not only to account for the existence of consciousness but perhaps even more so to account for its origin.

Where Did We Get THAT?

When it comes to the soul and consciousness, we must ask what would be the likelihood of consciousness arising from unthinking matter. As with so many of the happenstances of naturalistic evolution, the chances of it would be very, very, very (at *least* very [3]) slim.

Atoms that make up the universe are not conscious, so somehow consciousness has to be introduced into the system. In the larger scheme of the cosmos, consciousness is an oddity. What we observe are small outposts of consciousness in the midst of an over-whelmingly unconscious material universe. Consciousness is such an exceptional thing relative to unconsciousness that it should not be expected to exist. Yet, not only does it exist, even the unwitting material world gives the impression of having been programmed to operate in certain ways. At the risk of backtracking to our discussion of design, there appears to be design behind the forces of nature. Somehow, we have become able to perceive with our own design an apparent design in the unconscious forces around us.

This is an especially quirky aspect of reality when we bear in mind that these things that reflect design are not aware of themselves. As impressive as many forces of nature are, they do not know they exist. A tornado can't strut about how big and bad it is as it roils through town. And hurricanes don't appreciate their own capacity for destruction as they wipe out coastal cities.

The whole biosphere and its delicate balance of plants that produce oxygen and animals that generate carbon dioxide does not know itself.

Yet in the midst of this great mass of unconsciousness, you and I are conscious beings. Not only do you know yourself, but you also know these impersonal forces of nature and recognize design in them!

Did living things come into existence and then develop consciousness, or did consciousness come first? This is another of those questions that's not easy to answer. It's difficult to imagine consciousness coming to be before a living thing erupted from the ooze, but on the other hand, if we say consciousness evolved over time, it is difficult to figure how a nonconscious living thing could respond to its environment and survive until it became conscious. On top of that, we would be saying that intelligence and consciousness derived from nonintelligent material through undirected physical processes. It's like trying to determine whether the egg or the chicken came first; we're trying to figure out when the hidden pea of consciousness came into the picture.

The only real solution is to say that consciousness came about with existence, but that is at least as knotty a problem for naturalists as the irreducible complexity of a cell. In fact, it's really another variation on the problem of complexity. If the two things must coexist, it exponentially escalates the improbability that both could have come about at random. However, if we understand that God made the pea when he made the egg, it changes the whole thing. Because God has always been, he has always existed, and he has always been conscious. So for him to imbue a living being with consciousness at the time of creation makes sense.

Consciousness and existence would have had to start at the same time, and with God as Creator, that is a possibility. Lest we think a naturalist's problem with this issue isn't as great as I make it out to be since animals are less sophisticated than humans (and according to evolution they came about long before we did), bear in mind that it's not just humans that have consciousness. Every living animal exhibits a consciousness.

An animal has a body, and it also has a form of consciousness. While there are differences between animal consciousness and human consciousness, animals are nevertheless a quantum leap beyond plant life in this regard. Some naturalists point to animal consciousness to negate the argument for the existence of God as if we are saying that it is specifically human consciousness that points to God. But the consciousness argument proposes that any consciousness whatsoever is sufficient to point to God. Whether there is consciousness of an amoeba, a chimpanzee, a crawdad, or a vampire bat, naturalists have some explaining to do about where it came from. Evolutionists have a hard time explaining any kind of consciousness. But they try of course.

A theory called emergent evolution is the metaphysical sleight of hand used by naturalists to address this point. The concept suggests there is a hierarchy in levels of naturally existing information that build on each other. It starts with physics and moves on to chemistry. While mere physics does not explain all the complexities of chemistry, its laws give rise to the chemical interactions necessary to produce life and all its associated properties. Chemistry, in turn, provides the foundation for biology, and the principles of biology lead ultimately to anthropology. As this natural hierarchy spun into motion, the development that happened brought about life that allowed, somewhere along the way, for consciousness to begin and grow all the way up the life chain. However, if we pay attention to what's being said here, we'll recognize that it is not an explanation of origin but is, rather, just a description of what we find in the world—that both complex and "simple" animals have consciousness. The theory says *that consciousness did arise* (a statement of the obvious), but it offers nothing about how.

To drive home the point, let me digress to a more detailed example of the wonder of animal consciousness. Consider a dog. This animal has certain sensory perceptions that far surpass yours and mine. Dogs can hear a significantly wider range of sounds than we can. Blow a dog whistle, and you'll see what I mean. While you won't hear a thing, your dog will take note. These creatures also have a remarkable sense of smell, and whether sound or scent, dogs are conscious of the input they receive, and they react to it. Consciousness is at work. The same is true of birds and reptiles, and even fish are aware of their surroundings. Certain traits of consciousness go all the way down to bacteria.

The Ultimate Gift

The best way to know a human is conscious is that we have experienced it. Consciousness is like an amazing gift we discover without knowing exactly where it came from.

Imagine that you wake up one morning and find in your front yard a fully functional spaceship. And let's suppose you take the spaceship for a ride to the moon and that a friend rides with you. Along the way, your friend asks, "Where did you get this?" To which you reply, "I don't know. I found it in my yard." Your friend is astonished! It's hard to imagine anyone merely happening upon a spaceship, but it is obvious that the spaceship is real so it must have come from somewhere. If, however, you go on to claim that the spaceship merely happened—that it evolved through random occurrences in your front yard—your friend would likely (and rightly) think you are crazy. The appearance of the spaceship would lead any rational person to conclude that someone made it, and that completely logical deduction would lead to yet another, even greater question: *Why* did someone give you a spaceship?

The Greater Question

If consciousness just happened or, if it is merely an illusion, then the question of why we are conscious makes no sense. At best, consciousness is simply a biological tool that allows a living thing to adjust to its environment—a survival mechanism. But we've examined the difficulty of believing it simply happened, and the idea that consciousness is not real is likewise untenable. So we are left with a legitimate question of *why*. Why are people conscious?

Since naturalism has no reason even to consider the question, we'll turn again to our nonnaturalistic source for an answer. The Bible tells us that the soul—the seat of human consciousness—has the ability to connect us to God. As we saw earlier in this chapter, Jesus said each person's soul is going only one of two places. The possibilities are heaven and hell. An atheist says, "Oh no, I can't go to hell because I don't have a soul." But denying the existence of something does not change the reality of its existence.

Douglas Adams was well known as the author of a quirky series of books, the first of which is called *The Hitchhiker's Guide to the Galaxy*. The third in his series is a funny—if a bit weird—book entitled *The Restaurant at the End of the Universe*. In it, Adams presented a group of time travelers who, through some sort of cosmic accident, find themselves at the end of time. When they arrive at the termination point, they discover a classy, upscale restaurant. Assembled at the restaurant are dignitaries from all over the world, from every nook and cranny of history. They have gathered to witness the final explosion of all time and space.

While awaiting the end, these people encounter an android that has a computer brain the size of a planet, and they ask this brilliant machine the question: "What is the fundamental answer to the universe?" The android runs an array of calculations and replies, "Forty-two." "So," the assembled throng wonders, "if 'forty-two' is the fundamental answer to the universe, what is the fundamental *question*?" It is that question they spend most of the book trying to figure out.

People in real life ask the same question. It comes from that nagging pea under all the layers of who we are. What is life all about? Why am I here? Naturalism cannot account for wondering about our existence. Did you merely arrive here with a supercomputer in your head, wired with alertness? Is that the real you? It's a better guess that it was put there intentionally rather than that it simply happened by chance. Hopefully now you can see that if you were to place a good bet on where consciousness came from, you'd put your odds on God.

Actually, that would be an even better wager than you might imagine, and I'll explain why in chapter 10.

CHAPTER TEN

Betting on God

Prosecution: *The prosecution objects to the defense's intent to use Pascal's wager. The argument improperly encourages jurors to decide this case on their own personal interests, rather than as neutral arbiters of the evidence.*

Judge: *I will note your concern for the record, but I will allow the defense to use the wager in its closing arguments. I will, however, instruct the jury that it is forbidden to consider the wager as actual evidence for the existence of God. It should be considered as background only. The God/ no-God verdict must be rendered solely on the factual arguments and evidences that have been presented in these proceedings. Nevertheless, the jury is free to bear in mind that the wager may have merit in determining one's personal response to the facts.*

In 1933, Charles B. Darrow invented a game that he played on oil cloth with family and friends at his kitchen table. It seems anyone who played fell in love with this game and its titillating promise of getting rich. When word spread, people began ordering copies, which Darrow assembled at home and sold for $4 each.

Eventually, Parker Brothers—the game company—heard about Darrow's invention and bought the concept from him. Since then, it has become the best-selling game in American history. More than 200 million have been sold, and it has been published in twenty-six languages in eighty countries around the world. Also the largest home builder in America, this game has seen more than 5 billion little green houses put up since 1935, and the national and world championships, just like the Olympics, are held every four years.

The game, of course, is Monopoly.

Edward P. Parker, former president of Parker Brothers, once credited the success of Darrow's game this way: "The magic of Monopoly lies in its ability to be able to clobber your best friend without doing any serious damage." [1] Monopoly offers the thrill of amassing a fortune, the adventure of dreaming big. Fifth-graders can own railroads. A neighbor may go to jail. A wife can seize all her husband's assets. A brother can send his sister into bankruptcy. What a game!

It All Goes Back in the Box

When I was a kid, I loved to play Monopoly, and I *hated* to lose. My archrival was my grandmother, also a fierce competitor (so fierce, in fact, that after she died, we discovered that the red dice with which she always beat everybody at Wahoo, her other favorite game, were loaded). She was vicious, but I studied her weaknesses, and one day it happened. I drove my grandmother into the ground. I took her down, took everything she had! I watched in near delirium as she mortgaged her last property and gave up her last dollar—to me. I was nowhere near savoring the victory when she commanded solemnly, "Put it back in the box." Even though I wanted to bronze the game board, I obeyed and put it away.

For nearly ten chapters now, we've been talking about two sides of the most important question in the universe. The "prosecution," as I've called it, contends that this life is all there is, and when it's over, it's over. There's no God of eternity welcoming us anywhere. When one's earthly life is done, no matter how gloriou the achievements, how massive the fortune, or how fulfilling the personal era may have been, we simply put it all back in the box, and that's the end of the story. Everything one holds valuable—successes, loved ones, investments—is done with. On the other hand, the "defense" in our case contends there is a God who doesn't just put us all in a box and forget about our lives. There is an afterlife, sponsored by God.

Even though the subject of this chapter is not, strictly speaking, evidence for the existence of God, it does present another way to evaluate one's personal belief about the great truth of God's existence. The defense argues that when we believe in God, we are not believing in emptiness or nothingness but in something of substance based on evidence. Although some deride that mind-set as mere faith, the premise of this book is that such a faith is clearly an intelligent stance. And if you harbor even the slightest doubt based on the evidences presented, pay close attention to this chapter's short course on taking a gamble that can pay off forever.

Chances Are . . .

In Matthew 16:26 Jesus raised a haunting question: "What will it benefit a man if he gains the whole world yet loses his life?"

Risk analysis is an intriguing contemporary field of study, useful for a variety of business, military, and governmental purposes. At the Harvard Center for Risk Analysis, researchers study the science of risk and, among other things, analyze the chances of various happenings. In the process, they've come up with astounding statistics about things that could happen to us. Here are some of the odds:

· that you will ever be killed by a shark—one in 350 million
· that you will win the U.S. Powerball lottery—one in 80 million

- that you will win the Texas Lotto—one in 15 million
- that you will die in an earthquake—one in 11.2 million
- that you would ever be elected president of the United States—one in 10 million
- that you will die from a bee sting—one in 6 million
- that you will ever be struck and killed by lightning—one in 4.2 million
- that you will be electrocuted—one in 250,000
- that you will die by being murdered—one in 18,000

And of the five *leading* causes of death in America, here are the chances of dying from each different one:

- fifth leading cause, diabetes—one in 4,300
- fourth, emphysema and chronic lung disease—one in 2,400
- third, stroke—one in 1,750
- second, cancer—one in 514
- first, heart disease—one in 3842

In fact, the odds that you will die from *anything* this year are 1 in 117. Considering it's a life-or-death issue, that statistic suggests you could die at anytime. But here is the most sobering statistic of all, confirmed by Harvard and every other risk evaluator in the world: The odds that you will die at sometime in your life are one in one. That means death will happen to you and everyone else.

Like it or not, this brings stark focus to the question of an afterlife, which, as we've pointed out, is closely related to the question of God/no God. It was the burden of this question that prompted a gifted and creative seventeenth-century French scientist and mathematician to wonder if it is possible to determine the odds that God exists.

The God Odds

Blaise Pascal is regarded as the father of modern probability theory even though he lived a relatively short life (1623–62). Pascal grew up in Paris and was recognized as a genius even as a child. He wrote his first scientific paper at the age of eight. At sixteen, he wrote a mathematical essay on the sections of the cone that broke new ground in the field of geometry. At nineteen, he invented the calculating machine, a staggering discovery that was the forerunner of the modern computer, and by twenty-three, he had made major discoveries in physics and proven the existence of the vacuum beyond the earth's atmosphere. He also invented things—the syringe, a hydraulic press based on principles that came to be known as Pascal's law of pressure, and a much-improved barometer for measuring atmospheric pressure. He is probably best known, however, for his work on the calculation of probabilities.

Pascal was a skeptic who ended up placing his faith in Jesus Christ, largely because he applied the law of probabilities to God. His reflections and insights are found in a classic book called *Pensees*. In *Pensees*, Pascal explored a logical thought process about God's existence that has become known as Pascal's wager.

Pascal observed, "When it comes to the evidence for the existence of God you have a certain amount of evidence but in order to get to God you still have to cross a chasm by faith." [3] But Pascal was ready to help anyone make the move toward God. Since God rarely shows himself definitively, how, wondered Pascal, could someone make an intelligent decision about belief in the divine? He developed a mathematically precise decision matrix to help.

Pascal pointed out that the basic results from the thought process are really very simple: Either God is or he isn't. There is no middle ground. So Pascal constructed a wager. He developed four possible propositions and then considered the implications of each:

1. Bet God exists and he does exist.
2. Bet God does not exist and he does exist.
3. Bet God exists but he does not exist.
4. Bet God does not exist and he does not exist.

If you take bet 1, live appropriately, and you're right, that means you win big. You are kicking up gold dust in heaven for all eternity! But Pascal reasoned that if you take bet 2, you've bet against God, and you're going to hell. This is a serious loss indeed. Those two options are very clear cut, but here's where Pascal's wager becomes especially interesting.

What if you take bet 3? If you believe God exists, but he doesn't, you go back in the box. That's all you've won. You lose everything, but at least you've lived your life without worrying about going to hell. Not only that, you probably lived a better life—experienced love, peace, joy, and happiness—by following principles that enhanced the quality of your life on earth. But what if you take bet 4? Well, in the end, the result is the same: You go back in the box. You end up the same as the guy who lost bet 3, except that you didn't have the benefits of belief in God during your earthly life.

The Only Way to Win

Pascal concluded that the only way to win big is to bet on God, and the only way to lose big is to bet against him. Yet betting against him has no upside potential, only downside risk. Betting on God has an infinite upside but no worse downside than the best possible outcome of nonbelief. If you bet on God, you can't lose—it's a win-win deal—but if you bet against God, it's lose-lose. Pascal showed that the overwhelming odds favor wagering on God, and so the intelligent decision is to believe in

God and take Scripture seriously.

Although Pascal was not talking about a wager in the sense of gambling, we all make wagers at times that don't involve money. When we vote for a political candidate, for example, we are making a wager that he or she will represent us the way we hope to be represented. According to Pascal, though, even if the result isn't guaranteed, we have to make an intelligent decision based on our best reasoning about the anticipated result.

The Bible corroborates Pascal's wager. It teaches in no uncertain terms that we should bet on God because the payoff is great. If we bet on the divine and win, we live forever in heaven, a place the Bible says is so amazing we can't imagine anything better. (Unfortunately in talking about heaven, we sometimes make the big mistake of comparing heaven to church. Some people caution others, "If you can't sit in church, you won't like heaven." But oh my! I'm a preacher myself, and even I know church can be boring. Heaven is a million times greater than church.)

Another way to evaluate the benefits offered by Pascal's wager is to consider the pay-off in light of three inescapable, pertinent facts: life is short, death is certain, and eternity is long. Given these three immutable realities of human existence, how do we maximize our lives? It makes all the more sense to bet on God because the stakes are infinite. If God were to say that if we choose him he'll give us four extra lives, it would be worth it. Or three. Or two. Even doubling our potential life span would make it a good bet. But the potential payoff isn't only two or three extra lives—it is an infinity of extra lifetimes. The potential makes Powerball look like winning a coin toss and keeping the quarter. It's the difference between infinite loss and infinite gain.

This is why Jesus talked so passionately about the value of the soul. Even if anyone gained the whole world, it wouldn't be worth it at the price of his soul. The world would benefit him for only one lifetime, but his soul takes him through all eternity.

Like not thinking much about your brain, as I pointed out in the last chapter, too many people don't recognize the value of their souls. The reason we can't put an earthly price on it is that, when this life is done, the soul is the only thing that won't go back in the box. A soul ushers us into heaven…or not. It is a ticket to heaven if used properly. The Bible promises our souls will spend eternity in one of two places—heaven or hell. And spending it in the right place is worth more than a million worlds.

In this life, we learn it is often worthwhile to pay more for things that are durable. If we find a house builder with a reputation for building high-quality homes, we will pay the contractor more because the house will retain its value. Even in small things we find the same thing—the more expensive the flashlight batteries, the longer they last. We pay more for durability. And the most durable thing known is the soul. It goes on and on and on.

Another reason the soul is so valuable is that it is rare. Collector's items are worth more money. Gold is valuable because it's rare. The same is true of diamonds. Collectors know well the price of scarcity. The British Diana stamp is the rarest postage stamp on the planet. The rarest coin: Argenta of Athens. Rarest painting: Raphael's *Madonna*. There's even a rarest autograph in the world: Christopher Columbus's. Our souls are rare because we each have only one, and the value is inestimable because the "collector" wants them so badly. God desires our souls. He's placed an infinite price tag on each of us, and he also paid for it. John 3:16 says, "For God loved the world in this way: He gave His One and Only Son, so that everyone who believes in Him will not perish but have eternal life." Do you know who else desires our souls? Satan. It tells us something that God and the devil are after the same thing. Satan's not after countries or kingdoms

Those things don't last beyond this life, and they're not worth the investment of his time. Whatever he does to capture nations is only so he can get to the individuals that compose the group. He's after that much more valuable commodity: souls.

Satan even went after Jesus's soul. He offered Jesus the world, but Christ wouldn't give up his soul for short-term gain. Tragically, many people do make the trade. They exchange the eternal for the temporary. They sell out for money, pleasure, or worldly gain without the promise of a good payoff.

Our Very Own Risk/Reward Ratio

We've focused largely on the potential payoff with Pascal's wager to make the point that betting on God is the most intelligent way to go. But let's take a moment to consider the other side of the wager. What is the risk?

In modern terms we would call Pascal's thinking game theory. Now a field of study at many major universities, game theory can be applied to finance, contract law, risk management, bargaining, pricing, cost sharing, savings and investment, economics, and politics. The seminal book used in the field for more than sixty years is a monumental volume by John Von Neumann, *The Theory of Games and Economic Behavior*. This book supplies much of the basic terminology used in game theory.

Neumann defines *game* as a formal description of a strategic situation. One of the key components in playing is what is called a dominating strategy. Simply put, this is whatever you do that results in the best payoff. Another important term is *rationality*. A player is said to be rational if he or she seeks to play in a manner that maximizes his or her own payoff. In game theory, students are taught to play games rationally.

One of the most famous ways to teach the thought process is a game called "Prisoner's Dilemma." In the dilemma, two prisoners are held as suspects in a serious crime. Since there is very little judicial evidence for the crime, the state needs one of the prisoners to testify against the other. The one who testifies will be rewarded with immunity from prosecution while the other will serve a long jail sentence. However, if *both* testify, they will both go to prison but will serve only short sentences. If neither testifies, they will likely be in prison but will be taking their chances on how long the judge will make them serve—it could be a long time.

So what must the prisoners consider in order to determine whether or not to testify? The course of action that emerges is that to testify offers a higher payoff regardless of what the other prisoner does. While this theory has been applied to a remarkable array of issues—the arms race, litigation, environmental pollution—the key teaching of "Prisoner's Dilemma" is this: It is considered rational behavior when a player's fear of punishment outweighs the alternative. That's the smart way to play the game.

Most of us play "Prisoner's Dilemma" all the time, only we call it insurance. In this game, we bet the insurance company we're going to need certain compensations while the insurance company bets in return that we will not. With insurance, we "hedge" our bets, protecting ourselves so that we minimize the bad outcome of problems that may arise—wrecking a car, the house burning down, or being hospitalized with cancer.

This is a small picture of the big "insurance" game we play with death. As I said earlier, one's chances of dying someday are one in one. We all know how the game ends. Meanwhile, it's important to play by the rule book. The book of Genesis offers an intriguing narrative of death. Everyone whose story is recorded in that book ends up dying. In fact, the last words in Genesis are: "Joseph died at the age of 110. They embalmed him and placed him in a coffin in Egypt" (50:26). "A coffin in Egypt"—that's how the story ends that began in a paradise in Mesopotamia. It all went back in a box. And the same ending happens over and over again throughout the Bible. People die. Everyone dies. Why? Romans 3:23 and 6:23a have the answer: "For all have sinned and fall short of the glory of God," and "The wages of sin is death." The reason all die is because of sin. So here's how "Prisoner's Dilemma" applies: we've sinned, and because of that we all die. But we can receive a free gift that will negate death and allow us to live happily forever.

The question becomes, then, what are you going to do? You have three options. First, you can bet on God. The payoff if you're right is stupendous. Or you can bet against God, which comes with a gigantic downside risk if you're wrong but little reward even if you're right. Or you can choose not to bet. A lot of people try this strategy. But the rule book says that not betting is the same as betting against God (Luke 11:23—"Anyone who is not with Me is against me"). So if you decide not to bet, and God does exist, you lose just the same as if you'd bet against God. Therefore, the risk is the same as the no-God bet: No upside payoff, huge downside risk. No matter how you slice it, the only smart decision is to bet on God. Perhaps the most encouraging part of betting on God is that you can't go wrong. Still, many people just don't get it.

Six Reasons People Make the Wrong Bet

Despite the odds that favor the God exists bet, many people still maintain various objections. I've addressed a number of them below:

1. "I don't like the game, and I don't want to play." Whenever someone says he doesn't like the game, it means he's playing the game to lose because, like it or not, everyone is in the game.

2. "I want complete proof before I'll take this wager." Wanting complete proof is a smoke screen. Everyone knows there's no such thing. But in a court of law, as we've held throughout this book, proving something beyond a reasonable doubt is sufficient for much less weightier matters than the eternal destiny of a person's soul. And after we've considered enough evidence to eliminate all but unreasonable doubts, what's left is a relatively small step of faith.

Hebrews 11:6 says, "Now without faith it is impossible to please God, for the one who draws near to Him must believe that He exists and rewards those who seek Him." Many skeptics think they should somehow be able to come all the way to God without any faith. It is important here to distinguish between two things: proof and faith. Many atheists take the attitude, "If I had enough evidence, I would have faith." The problem is, if God materialized in front of you right now, that would nullify your will—something God won't do. Your mind wants the proof, but your will has to make a free choice about God. You see, God is more concerned about a person's will than about his or her mind. God has provided enough evidence to convince the willing and to condemn the obstinate. So what this objection is really talking about is the standard of proof.

Pascal believed that God is simultaneously hidden and revealed. Some people see him, and others can't. According to Pascal, "God is more proof to the humble, the humble get more, but the arrogant get less. They can't see it."[4] The Bible explains it similarly: "God resists the proud, but gives grace to the humble" (James 4:6b). God will not override your mind because that would overwhelm your will. That's why, once the evidence is in, people must come to God by faith.

3. "I can't believe; I'm not capable of believing." Smoke screen again. There's a big difference between "can't" and "won't," but people somehow think they can get away with it if they're unable, so they admit to "can't" but not to "won't" as a way to avoid responsibility. The real issue is that they are not open to the evidence.

Let's say you are in a totally dark room, and you need light. To get it, you have to open the door so light will come in. Open farther, and more light shines your way. You have to be willing to let the light in if you want to get out of the darkness. Close-minded skeptics who won't even examine evidence say, "I can't believe" when they've never studied, never openly tried to seek God.

4. "If I believe based on the wager, I would be believing out of the wrong motive—just to avoid hell." On this point, I have to admit the skeptic has it at least partially right. Pascal agreed that a person shouldn't believe just in case, simply to have fire insurance. The Bible (the rule book) also requires authentic conversion. You have to repent honestly of your sins and place your faith in Jesus Christ. But there's no reason Pascal's wager can't move someone toward a genuine faith.

5. "I don't want to do the wager because I don't know which God to bet on." Some dismiss Pascal's wager by accusing Christians of making it look like a 50/50 chance—we know God is or he isn't (that is our position, by the way). Skeptics muddy the waters, though, by saying there are religions and cults with differing interpretations of God, so the odds are not really 50/50. The various choices skew the possible outcomes. To which I answer, "Not so!" This is a philosophical shell game in which the atheist pretends he or she might believe in God. Game theory calls this a false

dilemma because if he or she disbelieves all, it is meaningless to pretend to believe in the possibility of many gods.

What makes it an even more tenuous position is that no religion other than Christianity even offers a wager. No other approach to God teaches that we can come to God as readily as Christianity presents. Simply saying there are false gods does not excuse a person from making a decision about the true one.

6. "I'm just not going to wager." Remember our most profound statistic of all—one in one? Death makes the wager work. As we've said before, whether you like it or not, you are in the game. If you're alive, the ship has already left port, and you're on it. Eventually the voyage will end. Put another way, God offers people a marriage proposal of sorts. If Harry asks Sally every week to marry him, and every time Sally says, "I'll let you know," one day Sally will die without ever having married Harry. People have been placed in this life to make a serious decision about God, and not to bet is to bet against him.

Remember, I said earlier in this chapter that Pascal's wager is not a proof for the existence of God, and Pascal never meant it to be. It offers, rather, a way of deciding how to make an intelligent decision about the God/no-God question and a way to take advantage of the situation if at the end of life, it doesn't all simply go back in the box. Pascal helped us calculate the odds and shows clearly the best bet is that the Divine One really exists and that he rewards those who seek him.

Reaching a Verdict

Y ou're the jury.

Does the evidence show you and every other reasonable person that God does, in fact, exist? And for you personally: Do you bet on God or against him? Every trial ends with closing arguments before the jury makes its final decision, so let's review evidence in the case for God and think for a brief but significant moment about what that means to you.

The Rest of the Defense

We first explained the evidence from desire in which every authentic need corresponds to a real way to meet it—there's food for the hungry. Since every innate desire corresponds to a real object and since every person has a desire to live forever, that desire must correspond to something that will fulfill it. You and I were made for another world.

With the evidence from conscience, we noted that something in all people tells them right from wrong, that a real sense of right and wrong is hardwired into human beings. This moral standard comes from somewhere, and the best guess is from an ultimate moral lawgiver.

In our observation about common consent, we saw that the vast majority of people in all places and in all times have believed in God. Is it likely that they're all wrong? Strictly speaking, they could all be wrong, of course, but that's not the most logical conclusion. A better guess is that these people all sense something that is real.

"The heavens declare the glory of God" (Ps. 19:1) was the essence of the argument from cosmology. How true it is! And the anthrophic principle bears out that everything in this universe is made for the good of man. *That* wouldn't happen by accident.

The evidence from design showed that for every conceivable design, there is a designer. A watch doesn't emerge from nowhere. Someone designed and made it. Why should the universe, the greatest design known, be any different? Naturalists' mumbo jumbo notwithstanding, there's every reason to think someone big designed the cosmos.

The argument from cause may have offered the most obvious thought process. Every effect requires a cause. Cause and effect is a phrase we use often because it is so rooted in everyday reality. Since science has determined the universe is not infinitely old, it must have had a beginning. Something caused it.

The argument from contingency pointed out that everything in this world is dependent and contingent on other things. But contingency absolutely must start somewhere with a noncontingent something. The only possibility is an eternal God.

With the evidence from miracles, if even one miracle has happened—just one!—God exists because God is the only being who could work miracles. The nonbeliever Josephus, the great first-century historian, credited Jesus with miracles. And he wasn't alone. Remember our formula: if evidence indicates that miracles have occurred, God must exist.

Then there's our own consciousness. The naturalist's explanation for its origin is based on the illogic that nonconscious stuff became conscious. But nothing in our experience suggests that anything conscious derives from something that is not. Another consciousness had to start it all.

The Prosecution Is Stringing Us Along

On the other hand, the prosecution presents little more than a string of absurdities. Something came from nothing. Spontaneous generation produced life from non-living matter. There is no real right or wrong, only social conveniences. Macroevolution must have happened even though no fossils or any other evidence suggest it did. The universe is one gigantic effect that has no cause. Even though things around us seem designed for a purpose, the appearance of design is a randomly generated illusion created by mindless forces.

No substance here. Nothing but wistful claims.

Four Simple Truths to Bet Your Life On

The truths of this case can be boiled down to four very simple, inescapable observations:

1. The evidence for the existence of God is far superior to the evidence for atheism.
2. The potential payoff for believing in God is infinitely huge.
3. The downside risk from believing in God is miniscule.
4. The downside potential of not believing in God is very bad.

Would you want to lose the bet on God? I hate to lose anything, and that's one I'd want to win at any cost. A popular bumper sticker captures the situation perfectly: "If you're living like there is no God, you'd better be right."

Jesus summarized the scenario of a bad bet. He said the best a person can hope for with a bet against God is to "gain the whole world." But think about that for a minute. First, no one has ever gained the world. Many have tried, but we see how the Caesars, Hitlers, and Saddam Husseins ended. Despite their immense, maniacal expenditure of power, they didn't even come close. Second, even if we could gain it all, it wouldn't satisfy us because it is temporary. It all goes back in the box. The bottom line is we can't win with this strategy. And not only that, it exposes us to enormous risk.

Without God in your life, you'll be dogged by the feeling you've made a bad bet. I remember what it was like to have that cloud over me, knowing that if I died at any moment, I just might go into an eternity in which there is a God I would have to face. It was a sickening feeling. On the other hand, even a Christian might think, *If I believe in God but he's not there, no big deal; I've had a good life in the meantime.*

Pascal's wager should haunt anyone who hasn't made the most intelligent bet. It certainly will haunt you when you die if you haven't. When people are dying, they don't think about sports. They don't think about current events or movies. They worry over what we've been talking about in this book. If God exists, when you die you become a believer no matter what you bet on in this life.

While God could randomly select the people to go to hell, he doesn't. Instead, he leaves that choice in our hands—a choice that one out of one of us has to make. Some people reading this book may not place the right bet. I hope I'm wrong about you, but let me remind you what this is all about: it's your verdict. That's why I positioned you as the jury for these findings. So you have to decide one of two things: Do you really think it all goes back in the box? Or does a God who exists see to it that after your life on earth, something else happens to you forever?

I can't decide for you. I can only decide for myself. I was once an atheist, but I decided to bet on God. And now I can tell you this: I'm not going back in the box.

NOTES

Chapter One: Innate Desires Point to God

1. C. S. Lewis, *Mere Christianity* (New York: Macmillan, 1952), 105.

2. Bertrand Russell, *A Free Man's Worship, Why I Am Not a Christian* (New York: Simon and Schuster, 1957), 107.

3. Cited by Peter Kreeft and Ronald Tacelli, *Handbook of Christian Apologetics* (Downers Grove, IL: Inter-Varsity Press, 1994).

Chapter Three: The Uncommonly Common Consent

1. Stéphane Courtois, *The Black Book of Communism: Crimes, Terror, Repression*, Mark Kramer and Jonathan Murphy, translators; Karel Bartosek, Andrzej Paczkowski, Jean-Louis Panne, and Jean-Louis Margolin, contributors (Harvard University Press, 1999; originally published in France, 1997); introduction, Martin Malia, U.S. edition.

2. Results available at www.gallup.com

3. Isaac Newton's *Principia*, 1687; Andrew Motte, translator, 1729; found in *The General Scholium*.

4. E. Salaman, "A Talk With Einstein," *The Listener* 54 (1955), 370–71.

Chapter Four: Cosmology—The Evidence "Out There"

1. Carman, "There Is a God," *R.I.O.T.*; copyright 1996, Sparrow Music.

2. Frank Harber, *Reasons for Believing* (Green Forest, AR: New Leaf Press, © 1998).

3. Jean-Pierre Luminet, Glenn D. Starkman, and Jeffrey R. Weeks, "Is Space Finite?," *Scientific American* (April 1999).

4. Galileo Galilei, letter to the Grand Duchess Christina, 1613.

5. Carl Sagan, *Pale Blue Dot: A Vision of the Human Future in Space* (Random House, 1994).

6. J. R. Gott III, "Implications of the Copernican principle for our future prospects," *Nature* 363:315–319 (1993).

7. D. Russell Humphreys, "Our galaxy is the centre of the universe, 'quantized' red shifts show," *TJ Journal of Creation* 16:2 (August 2002), 95–104.

Chapter Five: Design Is No Accident

1. Richard Dawkins, *The Blind Watchmaker: Why the Evidence of Evolution Reveals a Universe Without Design* (New York: W. W. Norton, 1996), 1, 91, 18.

2. An early concept of irreducibly complex systems comes from Ludwig von Bertalanffy, a twentieth-century Austrian biologist. (See Ludvig von Bertalanffy, *General System Theory: Foundations, Development, Applications* (New York: Allen Lane, 1971 [1968]).

3. Michael J. Behe, *Darwin's Black Box: The Biochemical Challenge to Evolution* (New York: The Free Press, 1998).

4. Charles Darwin, *On the Origin of Species by Means of Natural Selection, or the Preservation of Favoured Races in the Struggle for Life* (1859), 158.

5. Ibid., 155.

6. Ibid., 523.

7. Daniel Axelrod, *Science* 128.7 (1958).

8. George Gaylord Simpson, *The Evolution of Life* (Chicago: University of Chicago Press, 1960), 144.

Chapter Seven: Evidence from Contingency—It All Depends

1. Debate, Third Program broadcast, British Broadcasting Corporation, 1948. Reprinted in several sources, including Bertrand Russell, *On God and Religion*, Al Seckel, editor (Prometheus Books).

2. Mark Ridley, "Who Doubts Evolution?," *New Scientist* 90:1259 (June 25, 1981), 830–32.

3. Stephen Jay Gould, "The Return of Hopeful Monsters," *Natural History* 86[6]:22–30 (June-July 1977).

4. David B. Kitts, "Paleontology and Evolutionary Theory," *Evolution* 28 (September 1974), 467.

5. Steven Stanley, *Macroevolution, Pattern and Process* (New York: W. H. Freeman & Co., 1979), 39.

6. E. J. H. Corner, *Contemporary Botanical Thought*, A. M. MacLeod and L. S. Cobley, eds. (Chicago: Quadrangle Books, 1961), 97.

7. J. R. Norman, *A History of Fishes*, 3rd edition (New York: John Wiley & Sons, 1975), 343.

8. A. S. Romer, *Vertebrate Paleontology*, 3rd edition (Chicago: University of Chicago Press, 1966), 303.

9. Roger Lewin, "Bones of mammals' ancestors fleshed out," *Science* 212 (June 26, 1981), 1492.

10. Lyall Watson, "The Water People," *Science Digest* 90 (May 1982), 44.

11. See "Ecology," wikipedia.org.

Chapter Eight: Miracles, for Real

1. Amicus Curiae Brief for the National Academy of Sciences to the U.S. Fifth Circ. Court of Appeals, *Edwards v. Aguillard*.

2. *Modern History Sourcebook, David Hume on Miracles, Internet Modern History Sourcebook*; http://www.fordham.edu/halsall/mod/hume-miracles.html.

3. David Hume, "An Enquiry Concerning Human Understanding," in Richard Wollheim, *Hume on Religion* (London: Collins, 1963), 210–11.

4. Marie François Arrouet de Voltaire, *Dictionnaire philosophique* (Paris: Garnler, 1967), s.v. "Miracles."

5. Antony Flew, "Miracles," *Encyclopedia of Philosophy*, vol. 5 (New York: Macmillan and Free Press, 1967), 346–53.

6. *The Antiquities of the Jews* (book 18, chap. 3), *The Complete Works of Josephus*, William Whiston, translator (Grand Rapids, MI: Kregal Publications, 1981), 379.

7. David Hume, *Enquiries Concerning Human Understanding*, L. A. Selby-Bigge, editor, 3rd ed. (Oxford: Oxford University Press, 1975), 115.

Chapter Nine: The Wake-up Call of Consciousness

1. "Animal Consciousness," *The Stanford Encyclopedia of Philosophy*; http://plato.stanford.edu/entries/consciousness-animal.

2. Jaron Lanier, "Death: The Skeleton Key Of Consciousness Studies?," *Journal of Consciousness Studies* 4, 2:197, pp. 181–85.

3. Nick Herbert, Quantum Reality: *Beyond the New Physics* New York: Anchor, 1987.

4. David Chalmers, "The Conscious Mind," *Journal of Consciousness Studies* 2:3 (1995), 200–219.

5. Francis Crick, The Astonishing Hypothesis: *The Scientific Search for the Soul* (New York: Charles Scribner's Sons, 1994), 3.

6. Margaret Wertheim, "Scientists at Work: Francis Crick and Christof Koch; After the Double Helix: Unraveling the Mysteries of the State of Being," *New York Times* (April 13, 2004).

7. *The Emperor's New Mind* (www.wikipedia.org) states, "Penrose presents the argument that human consciousness is non-algorithmic, and thus is not capable of being modeled by a conventional Turing machine-type of digital computer. Penrose hypothesizes that quantum mechanics plays an essential role in the understanding of human consciousness. The collapse of the quantum wavefunction is seen as playing an im-portant role in brain function."

8. Peter Laslett, *The Physical Basis of Mind: A Series of Broadcast Talks* (Oxford: Basil Blackwell, 1950), 64.

9. Article on William Mayo, Associated Press, date unknown.

Chapter Ten: Betting on God

1. "Monopoly on fun," *The Albany Herald* (Friday, December 23, 2005).

2. "What, me worry?" *The Boston Sunday Globe* (November 11, 2001).

3. Blaise Pascal, Pensees, section IV, *The Means of Belief*, 278–79. "It is the heart that experiences God and not the reason. This, then, is faith: God felt by the heart, not by the reason. Faith is a gift of God; do not believe that we said it was a gift of reasoning. Other religions do not say this of their faith. They only give reasoning in order to arrive at it, and yet it does not bring them to it."

4. Ibid., 288. "Instead of complaining that God had hidden Himself, you will give Him thanks for not having revealed so much of Himself; and you will also give Him thanks for not having revealed Himself to haughty sages, unworthy to know so holy a God. Two kinds of persons know Him: those who have a humble heart, and who love lowliness, whatever kind of intellect they may have, high or low; and those who have sufficient understanding to see the truth, whatever opposition they may have to it."

Made in the USA
Monee, IL
09 September 2021